2018

SCULPTURE ON JAPANESE SWORD-FURNITURE

by
CAPTAIN F. BRINKLEY

Taken from
" JAPAN ITS HISTORY, ART & LITERATURE VII "

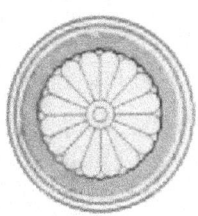

1902

SCULPTURE ON SWORD-FURNITURE

Of the three fields in which Japanese art may justly claim to have shown original genius, namely, the art of genre painting with its correlated achievements in chromo-xylog-raphy, the field of netsuke carving, and the field of sculpture as employed for the decoration of weapons of war, it is probably correct to say that the most remarkable work is found in the last. There is a common belief that the decoration of arms and armour did not reach a high grade of excellence until the twelfth century of the Christian era. Japanese traditions, on the contrary, allege that the inlaying of armour with gold and silver began in the fourth century, but there is nothing to support the assertion. The armour found in dolmens shows no trace of inlaying, or of any elaborate ornamentation, and it may be said that the contents of these peculiar tombs, which represent the burial-places of Japanese chieftains and sovereigns down to, probably, the fifth century of the Christian era, did not give much promise of the extraordinary skill afterwards attained. Nevertheless it is certain that the sculptor must have occupied himself diligently with the decoration of armour long before the Gempei wars of the twelfth century, for a suit of mail worn by *Yoshitsune*, the hero of that time, which is preserved in a temple at Nara, exhibits features of considerable decorative beauty. It is a combination of plate and chain defence, and the chiselling of the helmet, breastplate, and brassarts indicates that Japan possessed, at that comparatively early era, workers in metal not unworthy to rank with the sculptor of the Siris Bronzes. Indeed Yoshitsune's armour forcibly recalls that celebrated relic of the school of Praxiteles, for just as the Grecian artist adorned the shoulder-pieces of the armour with repoussé pictures of a combat between an Amazon and a warrior, so on *Yoshitsune*'s shoulder-pieces the Japanese craftsman affixed repoussé representations of the Dog of Fo, and on the helmet, flying pheasants. These adjuncts, however, are a minor feature in the case of the Japanese suit of mail. The chief characteristic is a wealth of designs — peony sprays, the well-known combination of plum, bamboo, and pine, chrysanthemum scrolls, and birds — in high relief, à jour, and in low relief. The craftsman who could execute such work had not much room for improvement, and indeed it is not surprising to know that a family which through many generations gave Japan her greatest artists in iron — the Miyochin family — was founded by an armourer, and had a celebrated representative in the second half of the twelfth century. While, however, this fine work was lavished on the decoration of armour certainly from the twelfth century and probably from an earlier date, the adornment of the sword did not receive commensurate attention until the fifteenth century, — a curious fact from the point of view of mere incongruity, but doubly curious when it is remembered that whereas armour was worn only on special occasions, the sword had a perpetual place in the girdle, and possessed, moreover, a value which seems romantic until something is learned of its really wonderful capacities. The sword itself, not being an object of art, will not be discussed here, great as is the interest otherwise attaching to it. What has to be spoken of is sword-furniture. There it was that the Japanese worker in metals won his crown of skill. In the decoration that he lavished on the guard, the hilt, and other parts of the sword's mountings, he gave to the world peerless specimens of sculpture in metal and of metallurgic processes. There is nothing in the cognate work of any other nation that surpasses, perhaps nothing that equals, the masterpieces of Japan in this line. The scarabs of Etruria have been mentioned as in some degree parallel, just as the Tanagra statuettes have been classed with the netsuke. If it be permissible to place on the same artistic plane a terracotta figure cast in a mould and a carving in wood or ivory, then also it may not be extravagant to compare the pictures sculptured and painted — no other term can be justly used — on metal by decorators of Japanese swords to the intaglios of Etruscan gem-cutters. These are matters of taste not profitable to discuss, nor will any one who has had an opportunity of examining a really representative collection of Japanese sword-furniture experience the least difficulty in forming a final opinion. He will recognise that he is dealing with pictorial art applied to metal, and the longer he studies the subject the greater the charms it develops and the more numerous the surprises it affords. This eulogy is not intended to imply that there are to be found among articles of Japanese sword-furniture monumental specimens of decorative metal-work worthy to be classed with objects such as the silver altar of the Florence baptistery, the candelabrum of the Milan Cathedral, the mediaeval rejas of Spanish churches, and many of the other magnificent achievements of European artists in metal. The two classes of work are not comparable. One might as well place in the same category the dancing maidens of the walls of Herculaneum and the most delicate miniature paintings on ivory. It has, indeed, been asserted that the extraordinary labour of mind and hand lavished by the Japanese artist upon objects the biggest of which can be enclosed within a circle three inches in diameter, justifies the criticism that he belonged to a nation great in little things and little in great things. But if the Japanese sculptor of sword-furniture is to be accused of moral smallness because he applied himself to the production of tiny ornaments, the same charge may be preferred against Benvenuto Cellini, since so much of his fame rests on his enamelled jewelry. Whatever quality of mind the fact indicates, it is indisputable that the Japanese artist or art-artisan is the most conscientious in the world. He loves to expend the finest and most patient effort upon the least conspicuous portions of the object he ornaments, partly because loyalty to his art dictates such a sacrifice of labour, and partly because he thus enters a kind of noble protest against any suspicion of decorative ostentation which the beauty and richness of his work might otherwise suggest. That habit of craftsmanship is well illustrated in sword-furniture. The delicacy of chiselling and infinitely careful finish bestowed on every detail delight the connoisseur as much as they astonish him. Admirable as is the netsuke-carver's work, the art of the sword-ornamenter has greater range and freedom. That, indeed, is a necessary result of the well recognised law that the more direct and complete the imitation effected by any art, the less the range and the number of the phenomena it can imitate. The netsuke being, for the most part, a sculpture in the round, the actions, expressions, and accessories represented by it must be limited by the principles of stability and simplicity that govern the "space-arts;" whereas, in the decoration of sword-furniture, the artist may introduce a much wider range of objects and a much greater complexity of actions. The student of these beautiful creations finds that Japanese sculptors have exercised to the full their proper latitude of motives and methods. The carver of sword-furniture did, in fact, make "pictures" in metal; that is to say, pictures within the limitations found applicable to all Japanese pictorial art, wherein such subtleties of appearance as are due to the incidence of light and shade find scarcely any place. The Japanese samurai carried two swords in his girdle. They are spoken of collectively as dai-sho (long and small), and separately as katana (the long sword) and wakizashi (the companion sword, that is to say, the short sword). There were four other kinds of sword; namely, (1) the tachi (called also jintachi, or "war" tachi), a long curved blade carried by samurai of high rank; (2) the tsurugi, a straight, double-edged sword used in ancient times (the katana, the wakizashi, and the tachi were all one-edged); (3) the aikuchi, a dagger (without guard), used originally for stabbing or decapitating a prostrate foe, and subsequently worn by the samurai when the dai-sho were removed (as on entering a friend's house); and (4) the kaiken (lit. bosom sword), a dagger (without guard) worn by women. The furniture of the sword,—that is to say, of the katana and the wakizashi, — commencing from the top of the hilt, consists of — The kashira (tip) — a metal cap placed upon the top of the hilt (kashira literally means "head," and in this case is an abbreviation of tsuka-gashira, or the "head of the hilt"). The menuki (rivet) — a piece of metal placed under the wrapping of the hilt to improve the grasp. The origin of the menuki will be explained presently. A menuki being placed on either side of the hilt, these ornaments always occur in pairs and have decoration en-suite. The fuchi — a metal ring encircling the hilt immediately above the guard. The ornamentation of the fuchi and that of the kashira is always en suite. The tsuba — the guard. The seppa — a small plate through which the haft of the sword passes before entering the guard. The habaki — two flanges (forming a single piece), which grasp the sides of the blade immediately below the seppa. The seppa and the habaki never carry decorative designs of any kind, but are mentioned here for the sake of completeness. The kozuka — a knife inserted in the scabbard of the "companion sword" (wakizashi). The tip of the knife's hilt lies opposite an opening in the guard through which it is drawn when required for use. It is generally supposed that the term kozuka applies to the hilt only of the knife or dagger, the whole being called the kogatana (little sword). But by kozuka the Japanese understand the knife attached to the scabbard of a sword, and by kogatana any knife, such as that used by a wood-carver, for example.

The kogai — a skewer inserted in the scabbard of the "companion sword" (wakizashi), on the side opposite to the kozuka. The kogai, like the kozuka, is drawn through an opening in the guard. It thus results that the guard of the "companion sword" has always two oval holes, whereas the guard of the katana is either without these holes, or has them filled with removable plates. The kogai served the samurai as a kind of hair-pin for fastening on his official cap (kammuri). In time of war it was put to a different use, being thrust into the head of a slain adversary for purposes of subsequent identification so that the victor might claim the honour due to his prowess. The kogai sometimes takes the form of a pair of skewers. The Kurigata — an oval knob fastened on one side of thescabbard, and having a hole through which the pendent cord (sage-o) is passed. The sage-o, which is always a strong braid of silk, is twisted round the scabbard like a sword-knot, but its chief use is to tie back the long sleeves of the surcoat during a fight. In the case of the curved sword (tachi), however, the sage-o served to fasten the scabbard to the girdle. The soritsuno — a piece of metal fixed on the scabbard of the "companion sword" below the kurigata to prevent the scabbard from slipping (sori) in the girdle. The kojiri — a metal cap sometimes placed on the end of the scabbard. The furniture of the curved sword (tachi) has a different nomenclature from the above. Its various parts are as follows: — Kabuto-gane (lit.helmet-metal)— the cap on the hilt, corresponding to the kashira of the ordinary sword. Musubi-gane (lit. knot-metal) — a ring attached to the cap for the purpose of receiving a small knot. Tsuka-ai (lit. hilt-companions) — corresponding to the menuki of the ordinary sword. Ichi-no-asbi and ni-no-ashi (lit. the first foot and second foot) —two bands with rings encircling the scabbard to receive the sword-knot (*sage-o*). Shiba-biki — the lowest ring on the scabbard. Ishi-zuki — the "boot" of the scabbard.

In order to reach the standpoint from which the Japanese view these decorative objects, to learn how they were regarded by connoisseurs in the country of their manufacture, and to discover what aims the best artists proposed to themselves in chiselling them, it is desirable to translate the words of the author of the *Soken Kisho*, a critical writer whose treatment of the subject is full and appreciative: —

GENERAL REMARKS.

As a general rule it is not so difficult to judge the quality of the carving on a menuki, a kozuka, and so forth as to pronounce an accurate verdict on the quality of the sword-blade. One must commence by studying the chisel-marks on the works of the thirteen successive generations of the Goto family — the iye-bori, as they are called — until one has acquired a thoroughly clear perception of the characteristics of each master's style. This must be done with such diligence that in the end the distinguishing features of each artist's work can be recognised at a glance. Thus equipped, the amateur will, of course, be in a position to discriminate between the iye-bori work and that of all other sculptors. It is not enough, however, to be able to identify the mannerisms of the chisels. The informing spirit of the work and its art quality must also be earnestly studied. This is the shortest and only route to become a competent connoisseur. For the sculpture of a genius, whether he belongs to the iye-bori or not, is invariably permeated by a lofty spirit, whereas that of the artisan, whatever be its technical beauty, lacks elevation of tone and is consequently quite inferior. When once the connoisseur's mind is furnished with an intelligent standard of refined loftiness, there will not be the least hesitation in detecting any low or vulgar features presented by a work. The kozuka and kogai of the first Goto masters (iye-bori), as well as of the experts of early eras, invariably have the ground covered with fish-roe [nanako] diaper— that is to say, very small granulations like the roe of a fish. It was formerly a point of etiquette not to wear, on occasions of ceremony, swords of which the kozuka and kogai were without the fish-roe ground. Those having the ishime (stone-grain) ground or the ji-migakii (polished ground) were not considered suitable for such occasions. But among the works of the later iye-bori there are many that have not the nanako ground. It is to be observed that the fuchi and the kashira are not included in the rule. Note.— The fuchi and the kashira do not properly belong to the class of sword "ornaments," being, in fact, essential parts of the mounting. They form with the seppa and the habaki inseparable elements of the mounted sword. The term nanako derives from the resemblance that the microscopic granulations bear to fish-roe. In the language of old Japan, "fish" was "*na*", and this with the suffix "*ko*" (egg) made the compound na-no-ko, or nanako.

None of the early representatives of the Goto family (iye-bori) made a business of carving anything but kozuka, menuki, and kogai. Only from the time (1570—1631) of *Tokujo*, the fifth representative, did they occasionally sculpture fuchi, kashira, and tsuba. Specimens of their work in these latter lines are very rare, and should be correspondingly prized. In recent times it is occasionally found that a gold crest (coat of arms) originally chiselled on a kozuka or kogai of old make has been detached and fixed on the fuchi and kashira, or on the fuchi alone, or on the tsuba; and in other cases gold-plated crests or incised designs have been newly attached to, or cut on, the original ground. Such objects are very rare, nor would devices of the kind have been employed by the masters except in compliance with orders that could not be disobeyed. It is a saying of the philosopher *Amamori Hoshiu* that "*in art there are four grades, the inferior (heta), the skilled (kosha), the expert (jozu), and the master (meijin)*" and that "*the same classification applies to the conduct of the gentleman.*" In such wise, also, may be distinguished the merits of carvers. Adopting that principle in compiling this work, I have divided the carvers of sword-furniture into three ranks. Natural talent combined with the skill acquired by long practice constitutes the "master," who stands at the highest point of his art. Next comes the "expert," concerning whom, however, a triple subdivision must be made: namely, the expert who ranks next to and immediately after the master; then the expert who, though originally of "inferior" ability, has nevertheless by zealous and patient effort developed the skill which ought to be the aim of every student; finally, the expert who by conceiving and executing some attractive novelty, obtains the passing plaudits of a curious public, but whose works ultimately lose their charm and stand revealed as unworthy of lasting admiration. All artists that do not rise to the rank of "master" or "expert" may be classed as "common." There are certainly gradations among these last, but the sum of the matter is that they belong to the "inferior" order and are persons of vulgar endowments. In every art the idea is first conceived, and the hand thereafter moves in obedience to the mind. The loftier the mind, the nobler the execution. An artist who produces inferior work should be ashamed rather than proud. The connoisseur of art objects must apply the same principle in forming his judgments.

Nobility of mind, absolute impartiality, and entire disinterestedness are the three essentials of a sound critic. The old-time carvers set out by learning from their masters how to handle the chisel, and when they had acquired skill in the technical processes, they made their owndesigns and sought to develop a special style. Thus, even those that did not rise to the level of "experts" often produced works showing skill, force, and graces of composition. So degenerate, on the contrary, are modern carvers that if they find an old work of fine quality, they carefully copy it by taking an impression. But their unskilled use of the chisel easily betrays them, for their execution is invariably prolix and awkward. None the less when, after long toil and much pain, they have succeeded in carving, polishing, and colouring, they fondly imagine themselves great artists, and with consummate silliness inscribe their names on these productions, pointing the finger of scorn at other sculptors. It is with the carver as with the painter. The good pictorial artist, after acquiring a thorough knowledge of the uses of the brush as taught by his master, copies many fine old pictures and studies them earnestly, so that, when he comes to paint independently, he has always before his mind's eye a model showing the inimitably exquisite points of the great chefs-d'oeuvre of the past. But he never prostitutes his natural talent so far as to make slavish imitations. Thus every touch of his brush is eloquent of original talent, and the true critic cannot fail to detect the merits of his work. Very different is the practice of the "inferior" painter. His solicitude is almost entirely about the motive of his picture, scarcely at all about the brush-work. He is not versed even in the rudimentary art of using the "charred stick" (yaki-fude) to change the scale of a drawing, or to alter the shape of the figures. He prefers to make tracings of old pictures and to reproduce them with elaborate accuracy. There are not a few of these imitators, and the connoisseur, whether of painting or of sculpture, must needs be on his guard lest he deceive others as well as himself. One naturally supposes that men like *Joi, Somin, Toshihisa, Yasuchika*, and other masters, who, by giving birth to a glyptic style of their own, achieved world-wide fame, and whose doors were thronged by eager applicants for their productions, must have amassed much wealth. But it is impossible for a man to be great in art and mercenary at the same time.

The common craftsman, as he bends over his task, is for ever estimating the wage it will bring. Thus the taint of covetousness is inevitably transferred to his work, constituting a feature which becomes more and more repellent as time goes by, and finally banishes the specimen to some degraded shop of a dealer in old metal. The true artist, though conscious that he toils for a living, has his recollection of the fact effaced by love for his work. At times he will lay aside his chisel for months if he finds that his heart is not in his work. When the inspiration arrives, however, he becomes so completely absorbed in his task that he cannot bear to lay it aside, day or night, until it is finished. There is vitality in the result: it is surpassingly good. But if the question of gain be considered, it is found that although the productions of the master fetch a high price, the profit to him is not as great as that accruing from inferior work quickly executed and cheaply sold. The poet *Basho* says, "*Pity it is that the shira-uo* (a tiny river-fish of silvery transparency and almost colourless) *should have a price*." A great artist is injured when the price of his work is discussed: it should be above price. Business men would do well to lay this precept to heart: "*Only to accumulate gold and silver is to be their slave*." The true aim should be to develop an extensive trade and to achieve a great career, just as the artist cherishes and strives for the reputation of his art rather than of himself. The chefs-d'oeuvre of the thirteen Goto masters as well as those of other celebrities are, for the most part, treasured as precious heirlooms in the families that possess them. They seldom come into the hands of the dealer. On the rare occasions, however, when one of these gems does pass into a merchant's keeping, some one is always charmed by it, and has a great mind to buy it, but cannot readily persuade himself to pay the price, and so asks the dealer to let him keep it for a time, during which he privately consults the opinions of other dealers as to the proper figure. That man's chief aim is to come into cheap possession of a great work, and happily he is almost always disappointed. He does an injustice to the work. The nobility that gives greatness to an artist's efforts, the quality that brings genuine success to the trader, the appreciation that enables us to acquire fine objects of virtue — these things are inaccessible unless the mind be set upon a high ideal. Sometimes valuable master-pieces are found among specimens supposed to be common, and a fortunate discovery is called "unearthing a treasure" (horidashi). The discoverer boasts of it, but if he had true elevation of mind and refinement of taste, he would be above such pettiness. It is the luck of the mere trader.

TSUBA (Guard)

This term is derived from the name of a kind of cotton-spinning spindle which had a ring fixed on it. The tsuba of course existed from a very ancient epoch. It is mentioned in annals compiled in the eighth century, and is often spoken of as neri-tsuba (wrought-iron guard) (The present Editor notes "neri-tsuba" are always made of leather, often of several layers, sometimes reinforced with an iron or other metal rim or internal plate, thus the reference as "neri-tsuba" being of wrought iron is incorrect.) The sword of *Takauji*, preserved at Atago-san, has a guard of wrought iron, and in the Taira Annals (Taihei-ki) gold guards are referred to.

N.B. Sometimes a specimen which does not bear a name indicating that it belongs to the class of either iye-bori (carvings of the principal Goto family) or domyo-bori (carvings of the branch Goto families), but which is nevertheless of such fine workmanship as to suggest that it came from a master's chisel, is sent to the Goto family for inspection, and returned with a written statement, "found inferior on examination and not identified by us." The dealers call such specimens "rejects" (nagerareshi), and it is said that the Goto experts put a chisel mark — the gimmi-tagane — on all these pieces, so that they can be at once recognised if submitted again for examination, but where the mark is placed the family never divulges.

N.B. The double kogai (wari-kogai), which is usually decorated with carvings of a plum-tree and a brushwood fence, or of bamboo, flowers, and plants, generally goes by the name of tayukogai, because its reputed originator (Kahei) became a skilled singer and received the musical title *tayu*.

N.B. In the chiselling of the fish-roe ground (nanako) slight differences are observable between the works of the artists of Yedo, Kaga, Kyoto, Awa, and so on. A good judge of carving must be familiar with these differences, but it is useless to attempt any written description of them.

THE FOURTEEN GENERATIONS OF THE GOTO FAMILY

1. **Yujo** — the founder of the family, true name *Masaoki Shirobei* — held the title of "Sado-no-kami" (lord of Sado). A native of Mino, he served in a military capacity under the Ashikaga chieftain, *Yoshinori*. Born in 1439, he died in 1512, at the age of seventy-three. *Yujo* obtained many of his designs from the celebrated painter *Kano Masanobu*. He is regarded as the founder of the school of sword-decorators, and his works possess great value. He invented the style of chiselling called taka-bori (carving in high relief), and his work is almost supernaturally skilled. It may be compared to the "*exquisite view of Gobi's snow-clad peak towering lofty in the sky.*" (from a Chinese poet), or to the weeping-willow in the Imperial garden as it waves in the soft breeze, or to the lovely lotus in the fairy lake washed by pearls of dew. So elevated is the tone, so delightfully chaste the character, of the carving that one cannot look at it without emotion. The traces of the chisel are at once bold and delicate, and every part of the work stands out vivid and almost divine. *Yujo* may truly be called the "Saint of the Art."

2. **Sojo**, true name of *Takemitsu Shirobei*, was the son of *Yujo*. He received the art title Hogen. Born 1486; died 1564. His work resembles that of his father so closely as to be almost indistinguishable. The carvings of the two masters may be compared to the iris and the sweet flag, distinct plants which nevertheless bear a strong likeness to each other in colour, fragrance, and even time of flowering.

3. **Joshin**, true name *Yoshihisa Shirobei*, was the son of *Sojo*. Born 1511; died 1562. The marks of the chisel are sharp; the relief very high and the depression deep. It is strong work. In making a menuki of shakudo or gold, he beat it into the desired form, and then added the plating in colours. This method was called uchidashi (repoussé), and the addition of the coloured metals without fracturing the ground was known as uttori. This style obtained much vogue in Joshin's time, but is less fashionable now. The art of inlaying (zogan), as applied to sword ornaments, was also inaugurated by *Joshin*, and his productions are the most varied and peculiar of the iye-bori works.

His work may be compared to a brave warrior who is not only a strong guardian but also a trusty councillor; for while it has boldness and strength, it has also something of delicacy and softness. He bore a different art-flower, but the same fruit as his predecessor.

4. **Kwojo**, called also *Mitsuiye*, was born in 1530, and died in 1620. He was a son of *Joshin*. His work resembles that of *Yujo* in style. It is noble and dignified, neither too strong nor too weak. The impression it conveys is that of resting under the green shadow of a patriarchal pine and looking out on a glow of cherry bloom. Or it may be compared to a noble lady standing beside the brushwood gate of a rustic dwelling.

5. **Tokujo**, called also *Mitsutsugu*, was the son of *Kwojo*. Born 1549; died 1631. *Hideyoshi*, the Taiko, conferred an estate on him in the year 1580. His work has the characteristic of strong surface modelling, and many specimens are scarcely distinguishable from those of his father *Kwojo*. Looking at his designs, one is reminded of white sails scattered near and far over the wide bosom of the sea when the brooding breath of spring softens their outlines. It was in *Tokujo*'s time that the custom originated of issuing certificates of authenticity (orikami) with the works of the Goto family. One of his sons, *Chojo*, became the founder of a branch of the family known as the "Shimo-Goto" (lower Goto).

6. **Yeijo**, called also *Masamitsu*, the son of *Tokujo*, was born in 1574 and died in 1617. His work combines the finished skill of both *Kwojo* and *Tokujo*, and has, at the same time, a certain quality of richness, tenderness, and restfulness. One may find a comparison in the view of a little boy driving an ox to pasture on a verdant plain; or the carriage of a nobleman standing beside a rustic fence over which convolvulus blossoms cluster.

7. **Kenjo**, called also *Masatsugu*, was a son of *Tokujo*. He represented the family during the minority of his nephew *Sokujo*, and was promoted to the rank of Hokkyo. Born 1585; died 1663. His manner of using the chisel greatly resembled that of *Kwojo*. One is reminded of a pine-tree and a bamboo covered with snow: they present a delightful contrast, but at heart retain the same changeless green. The fidelity and chastity of his work force themselves into notice. During the Kwanyei era (1625-1643) • his services were engaged by the feudal chief of Kaga, who gave him a pension of 150 koku of rice annually (about 1,500 yen), and he made it a custom thenceforth to live in Kaga every second year.

8. **Sokujo**, called also *Mitsushige*, was the son of *Yeijo*. Born 1603; died 1631. His style resembles that of *Kenjo*, and is characterised by directness, strength, and vigour. Connoisseurs are wont to class the works of *Yujo*, *Kojo*, and *Kenjo* as the "three chefs-d'oeuvre" (sansaku), but specimens by *Sokujo* are exchangeable with those of *Kenjo*. There is a notion that something of the value attaching to *Sokujo*'s works is due to their rarity, for as he died at the early age of twenty-eight, his productions were not numerous. But that is a mistake. He was a veritable genius, and to that fact alone is due the esteem in which his carvings are held. It is believed by good judges that had he lived longer and attained the mastery of technique which many years of effort can alone give, he would even have surpassed his ancestors, and a sympathetic perception of his latent capacities has something to do with the rank accorded to him by posterity. In the same way connoisseurs often class the works of *Tsujo* (eleventh representative), *Sokujo*, and *Kwojo* as the three chefs-d'oeuvre, declining to include the sculptures of *Yujo*, whom they place in a rank by himself as a divine and matchless master. That is a point of delicacy.

9. **Teijo**, called also Mitsumasa, the son of Kenjo, was born in 1603, and died in 1673. He represented the family during the minority of his nephew Renjo. He was promoted to the art rank of Hokkyo. His works are at once charming, noble, and dignified. It is impossible to deny their title to be called masterpieces.

Though his time was not very remote from our own era (1781), his carvings have the peculiar aspect of age presented by the work of *Kwojo* and the other early masters. The chisel-marks are somewhat deep, clear, and strong. His designs suggest the feeling experienced when, looking out under the bamboo blinds from the upper room of a lofty riverside dwelling, one sees the moon rise on an autumn evening. This artist succeeded to the pension of his father *Kenjo*, and used to live in Kanazawa (chief town of Kaga) every second year. In the house that he inhabited there may still be seen a stone garden ewer with the figure of *Hakuga* (a Chinese poet) engraved on it by the chisel of *Teijo*. It is said that during *Teijo's* time the Goto family employed a number of Kyoto chisellers to do rough work.

10. **Renjo**, called also *Mitsutomo*, son of *Sokujo*, was born in 1626 and died 1708. His work is gentle and magnanimous in tone. It reminds one of the quiet, subdued style in which the story of *Akashi* is told by the author of the Minamoto Annals (Genji Monogatari). He lived to a ripe old age and had many pupils, so that his works are often found. A son of his called *Mitsuyoshi* gave promise of future greatness, but unfortunately died young and few specimens exist from his chisel.

11. **Tsujo**, called also *Mitsutoshi*, was the son of *Senjo* and grandson of *Teijo*. He did not belong to the elder branch of the family. Born in 1668, he died 1721. His works are classed among the "three chefs-d'oeuvre (san-saku)" His style is somewhat showy. One can almost smell the fragrance of the flowers he chiselled, his birds seem to be on the point of flying or in actual flight, and his human figures smile as though words hovered on their lips. His sculptures are in truth beautiful beyond expression. Chinese annals tell of a puppet presented by a certain artist to a great monarch, and describe how the figure sang and danced automatically. That was a mere mechanical contrivance for the amusement of the moment. Very different is the air of vivid vitality imparted to his sculpture by the master-artist. Though no actual motion to strike the eye of the common observer, there is a latent force imparting to everything the element of motion, and creates a precious picture to be forever esteemed and admired.

12. **Jujo**, called also *Mitsumasa*, son of *Tsujo*, was born in 1694 and died in 1742. His work differs from that of *Tsujo*. It resembles the best productions of *Mitsutaka*, the present (1781) representative of the family. One is reminded of a man reaching his goal by steadily treading the right road. There is also an element of balanced strength that suggests the fabulous serpent of *Jozan*, which could defend itself equally with either end.

13. **Yenjo**, called also *Mitsutaka*; son of *Jujo*, was born in 1720 and died in 1784. Criticised unreservedly, his works seem to vary in quality. The best are not unlike the productions of *Tsujo*, for which they may easily be mistaken. The lustre of his house is not tarnished, nor the long-sustained reputation of his family impaired, in his hands. Since the death of *Yujo*, the founder of the family, two hundred and sixty years have passed. During that time the works of the masters from generation to generation have found their way into the hands of the great and the noble, who treasure them as precious possessions, their value augmenting as time rolls on. That is because the art of the illustrious ancestor has been adorned by the achievements of his descendants, every one of whom was himself a master. These happy results are mainly due, however, to the peaceful sway by which we are blessed, and to the tranquil times when men have leisure to show their respect for the dignity of a sword by the decoration they lavish on its mountings.

14. **Keijo**, called also *Mitsumori*, son of *Yenjo*, was born in 1739, and is still living (1781) in the Kyobashi district of Yedo. The work of this artist has the beauty of his grand-father *Tsujo's* carving, together with the well-balanced arrangement of his predecessors. His style is his own. There is a tender suggestiveness about his designs that reminds one of a light shower sweeping across the verdant slope of a mountain, or a soft haze resting on the bosom of a limpid lake. His work always shows that noble elevation of tone which belongs to the true artist and can never be imitated.

N. B. Here follow facsimiles of the certificates orikami (lit. "folded paper") given by the Goto experts, but such documents convey no information to foreign readers, and, moreover, have been so often and so successfully forged that to distinguish the true from the false is now almost as difficult as to judge the qualities and identify the sculptor of the art objects to which they refer. The reader will agree that these commentaries from the pen of a Japanese connoisseur convey a truer and more trustworthy idea of the attitude of the Japanese mind towards the work of the sculptor of sword-ornaments, and, indeed, toward art in general, than could possibly be gathered from a foreign analysis. Even the most intelligent and least prejudiced foreign student has much, nay, insuperable, difficulty in tracing the exact processes of Japanese intelligence. The Japanese are quiet folks. They never expatiate upon beauties presumably as obvious to others as to themselves; never enter into perfervid disquisitions about the "features" of a natural or an artificial picture. To do so would be to slight the eloquence of the picture itself and to insult the intelligence of the observer. A Japanese collector, unless his habits of thought and speech have been radically modified by intercourse with Occidentals, will show the whole of his treasures — if, indeed, he can be induced to show them at all — without making, from first to last, the briefest comment on their "points." The sole exception is in the case of an object which claims the reverence of association, —an object once honoured by the ownership of some celebrated warrior, statesman, or litterateur, and hallowed by the "odile" [ko-taku] of his touch. Concerning the origin of such a treasure he will volunteer some information, its story being otherwise untraceable. But whatever is within the unaided reach of expert observation, he leaves to be observed. His silence has been greatly misinterpreted. The ordinary foreigner construes it as evidence either of undeveloped speech or of an unfurnished mind. Strange conclusions surely, the one involving the hypothesis that the silent vocabulary of a people's shaping art may be richer than the spoken vocabulary of the idealism informing that art; the other, the still more unreasonable assumption that a nation can be blind to the beauties of its own creation. *Michitaka*'s comments on the works of the Goto sculptors dispel all these delusions. Some of his comparisons may sound even extravagant.

They are not extravagantly expressed, however. Nothing could be simpler than the language in which they are couched. Nature speaks to the Japanese in words of clearest meaning. Other eyes drink in just as deep a draught of enchantment from sunset on —"the happy autumn fields"— or from moonlight bathing a cherry grove in spring; but it may be truly said of the Japanese that in the course of long centuries of refined civilisation, they have gradually grouped together nature's fairest combinations into a series of ideograms each of which has come to be intimately associated with conceptions and emotions which the physical aspects of the scene alone could not suggest or inspire. There exists a wide field of thought which, though open to poetry, is closed to the arts of manual imitation. But from what does poetry derive its special sway over regions of the mind that lie beyond the direct influence of imitative art? Is it not from its power of invoking from the recesses of the heart feelings and experiences to which the painter or sculptor can appeal only by accidental association? In Japan, however, poetry has so constantly and faithfully drawn its inspiration from nature's images, and has been so loyally content to limit itself to appreciated interpretations of their suggestions, that mere mention of a particular combination of natural beauties summons to Japanese sight a picture of concrete loveliness and to the Japanese mind a poem of abstract ideas. Thus, when *Michitaka* speaks of —"*a light shower sweeping across the verdant slope of a mountain,*" or of "*a soft haze resting on the bosom of a limpid lake,*" or of "*white sails on a wide sea, their outlines softened by the brooding breath of spring,*"— he knows that he is recalling to educated minds, not only delightful images, but also certain subtleties of artistic conception and certain shades of emotion which convey his meaning with accuracy such as no mere verbal analysis could achieve. The above remarks apply to the style and the technique only of the art. The author of the *Soken Kisho* seldom makes reference to decorative motives, unless a sculptor's fame is connected with some special departure in that direction. The quality of the chiselling is, in fact, the first point to which the Japanese connoisseur directs his attention. On the other hand, the decorative design is the prime object of the Occidental dilettante's admiration.

In " L'Art Japonais " that most appreciative critic, *M. Gonse*, says :
— *"One blushes quickly on the technical skill of the Japanese carvers, so much it seems to them a gift of nature; but one experiences an ever new enjoyment in the study of the decor itself. What tact, what flexibility! As both sides are so harmonious! Because, very often, the subject continues on the face and the reverse and presents in each of these parts the same interest. Sometimes he rides on the big and the little sabers. We will see Shoki, on the great guard pursuing the devil hiding on the little one; in one, Komachi seen as young and beautiful; in the other, old and bowed by age, &c. The study of the microcosm of this art could lead to infinity."* —

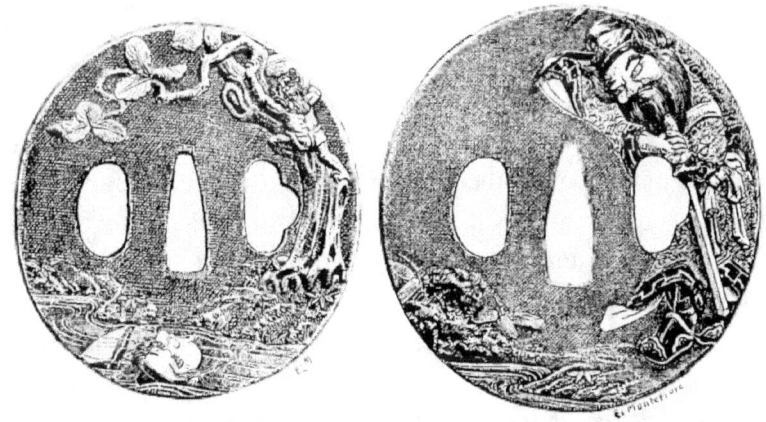

SHOKI IN PURSUIT OF ONI   DAISHO (PAIR)

The standpoint of the French connoisseur's eulogy is as far removed as possible from the standpoint of the Japanese themselves. The fact is that *M. Gonse*, who must be taken as representing the most intelligent class of Occidental students of Japanese art, rivets his attention on the work of the painter rather than on that of the sculptor; considers the pictorial motive in preference to the glyptic method. Now, as a rule with very rare exceptions, the decorative motives of Japanese sword-furniture were always supplied by painters. There exist innumerable volumes of designs from the brushes of more or less renowned artists, and to these the sculptor habitually referred for inspiration. All classes of art-artisans possessed such volumes, and were prepared to submit them for a customer's choice of motive. Hence it is that the Japanese connoisseur draws a clear line of distinction between the decorative design and its technical execution, crediting the former to the pictorial artist, the latter to the sculptor.

The enthusiastic eulogies and poetic comparisons of the *Soken Kisho* refer, not to the pictures chiselled on sword-guards, dagger-hafts, or hilt-tips, but to the manner of their execution. *Michitaka*, in common with all Japanese connoisseurs, detected in the stroke of a chisel and the lines of a graving-tool subjective beauties which appear to be hidden from the great majority of Western dilettanti. He never fell into the mistake of confusing the inspirations supplied by the decorative artist with the technical achievements of the sculptor himself. However elaborate may be the decorative design, however interesting the motive, the Japanese connoisseur never forgets to look first to the chisel work. By its quality alone he estimates the rank of a specimen, just as the critic of pictures judges the authenticity of a painting by the force, directness, and delicacy of the brush strokes. This becomes more easily comprehensible when it is remembered that vigour and grace of line-drawing are the prime essentials of fine art in the eyes of a Japanese, and that his almost instinctive appreciation of those qualities in a picture equips him with a special standard for judging the excellence of sculpture such as is found upon sword-furniture. The Japanese dogu-bori used thirty-six principal classes of chisel, each with its distinctive name, and as most of these classes included from five to ten sub-varieties, his cutting and graving tools aggregated about two hundred and fifty. This fact alone suffices to suggest the delicacy and elaborateness of his work. There are certain technical facts a knowledge of which is necessary not only to the connoisseur of sword-ornaments, but also to the student of Japanese metal work in all its admirable developments. In the first place, the nature of the metals employed has much interest, as well for the sake of the insight it affords into the metallurgical ingenuity of the Japanese as for its bearing upon this branch of the country's art. Japan did not at any time possess an abundance of gold. The principal source of supply was river sands, and in washing out the precious metal processes were employed which, though apparently rough, have been proved by Western experts to be profitably applicable to gravel yielding only six cents worth of gold per cubic yard. If the descriptions of Japan penned by *Koempfer* and other early writers were accepted literally, it would be necessary to conclude that gold was exceptionally abundant and profusely used for ornamental purposes.

But the truth is that although the Japanese loved the rich glow of the noble metal and utilised it largely in the adornment of temples, in domestic architecture, and for various ornaments and utensils, they thoroughly understood the art of making a little go a long way, and many objects which a casual observer might readily mistake for solid gold, were nothing more than gilded copper. Still, as the gold-leaf employed for gilding purposes was thicker than that serving the same end in the Occident, the quantity of the precious metal required for coating Buddhist images (whether of bronze or wood), temple utensils, and architectural ornaments must have been considerable. Table utensils of gold or silver did not exist, with the exception of cups for drinking wine and vessels for mulling it, together with small kettles, censers, and other minor objects to be spoken of by-and-by. For the manufacture of sword-ornaments, however, — especially menuki, — and pouch-mountings, pure gold was constantly used. Guards of solid gold are scarcely ever found, except in the case of the aikuchi (a short dagger-like weapon carried by the samurai and used to cut off the head of a fallen enemy). It is true that several collectors in Europe and America possess, among their art treasures, large tsuba (guards) of pure gold, ornamented with the utmost elaboration of detail. But these, with few exceptions, were made expressly for sale to foreigners, and never formed part of a Japanese sword. The term "pure gold " is not used here in an absolutely literal sense. In former times the Japanese were not familiar with the delicate assaying methods in vogue in the West, and could not determine the quality of cither gold or silver with the extreme accuracy attained at an American or European mint. They used a touchstone only, a small plate of black siliceous shale, but used it with such skill that their results — according to an eminent authority, *Mr. W. Gowland* — did not show a maximum difference of more than one per cent from assays made by Occidental methods. Their success with silver was not equally marked, but they were able to obtain it so pure that five hundred and fifty-five specimens of old silver assayed in recent years at the Imperial Osaka Mint were found to contain an average of 99.3 per cent of pure metal.

It is, perhaps, scarcely necessary to note that for manufacturing purposes pure gold or silver was never used, the former being alloyed with silver and copper and the latter with copper, not with the idea of debasement, but in order to obtain greater hardness and freedom from vesicular cavities when casting. If, however, the Japanese metallurgist possessed and practised highly skilled methods of freeing the precious metals from impurities, he was also remarkably clever in "surfacing" either gold or silver so as to obtain an appearance of absolute purity. The question here is not of patina, — a legitimate and beautiful feature which Japanese craftsmen had exceptionally ingenious devices for imparting to all the metals used in objects of art, — but to a process originally elaborated in connection with debased coins, and sometimes resorted to by art-artisans of low class, though no kinzoku-shi (gold-smith) of repute ever descended to such deception, — a process of dissolving out the impurities from the upper layers of a gold or silver alloy until the surface assumed the appearance of pure metal. Gold and silver, though here spoken of in some detail, played a subsidiary rather than a principal part in the manufacture of sword-ornaments, being used chiefly to pick out the details of the decorative design. The ground metals were iron, copper, and, above all, shakudo and shibuichi, two alloys invented by the Japanese and never used by any other people. Owing to the great beauty of the patinas that can be given to them, these alloys are uniquely excellent for art purposes. Shakudo (literally, "red copper") is an alloy of gold with excess of copper, the approximate proportions being three per cent of gold to ninety-seven of copper. The alloy, when it emerges from the furnace, presents no special features, being simply dark-coloured copper. Its value for artistic purposes depends on the fact that a glossy black patina with violet sheen may be produced on its surface by suitable treatment. *Mr. W. Gowland*, who has devoted special research to this subject, says: —The alloy has been long known to the Japanese, but there are no records of its first use, and the date of its origin cannot be even approximately determined. Perhaps the least doubtful of the earliest specimens known to us are the mounts of the sword of *Ashikaga Takauji*, who held the position of Shogun from 1335 to 1337, which is preserved in the temple of Itsukushima.

There may be earlier examples, but it was certainly not known in the ninth century. The oldest specimen of Buddhist art-metal work in the decoration of which shakudo appears, so far as I have been able to trace, is a reliquary containing fragments of the bones of St. Nichiren in the famous temple of Minobu (date 1580). In many temples there are statues of divinities and saints which are said to be composed of this alloy, but those I have had the opportunity of examining were all of ordinary copper-tin-lead bronze. In the seventeenth century it was extensively employed, but the finest examples of it as a decorative alloy are found in the guards and other furniture of the swords of the last century and the first half of the present. The addition of gold to bronze in order to obtain a black patina has been long known to the Chinese. It is hence possible that the Japanese may have learned from them this peculiar property of gold; but the pure alloy of copper and gold, of the true shakudo, is essentially Japanese, and is unapproached in the beauty and richness of its patina by any alloy of the Chinese, either of old or recent times. Its rich deep tones of black, and the splendid polish which it is capable of receiving, render it alike a perfect ground for inlaid designs of gold, silver, and copper, and for being similarly inlaid in them. This alloy, too, possesses physical properties which are of extreme importance to the worker in metals, and enable him to manipulate and fashion it as he desires. It can be cast into any form; can be hammered into sheets and drawn into wire. No large castings, however, have been made of it. The method by which the black patina is produced is as follows: The object is first boiled in a lye prepared by lixiviating [leaching] wood ashes; after which it is carefully polished, if necessary, with charcoal powder. It is then immersed in plum-vinegar containing common salt in solution, and, after being washed with a weak lye, is placed in a tub of water to remove all traces of alkali. After this treatment it is digested in a boiling solution of copper sulphate, verdigris, and water, to which sometimes potassium nitrate is added, and the desired patina is produced. It is roughly stated above that shakudo is composed of 97 per cent of copper to 3 of gold. But, in truth, no less than fifteen grades of the alloy are used by Japanese craftsmen. The lowest of them — called chiusho — contains only traces of gold, and the highest has as much as 7 per cent of the precious metal.

Analyses of seven specimens of shakudo made by Mr. Gowland, Mr. Kalischer, and Mr. Atkinson gave the following results: —

ANALYSES OF "SHAKUDO"

	Gold.	Silver.	Copper.	Lead.	Iron.	Arsenic.	Total.
1	4.16	0.08	95.77	—	—	—	100.01
2	3.75	1.55	94.50	0.11	Trace	Trace	99.89
3	2.67	2.06	94.90	0.11	—	—	99.74
4	2.45	1.24	96.00	0.06	—	—	99.75
5	1.52	2.01	96.10	0.08	—	—	99.71
6	1.00	1.37	97.40	0.07	—	—	99.84
7	0.49	0.29	97.04	—	—	—	99.82

Another alloy peculiar to Japan and of at least equal importance with shakudo for artistic purposes, is shibuichi, a term literally signifying "one part in four;" that is to say, one part of silver by weight to three of copper. That, doubtless, was the original composition of the alloy. Indeed Japanese records state definitely that the ordinary variety of shibuichi contained 10 momme (5.8 grs. Troy) of copper to 2% momme of silver. But, as a matter of fact, the shibuichi employed for sword-furniture and other artistic work was usually the kind known as sambo-gin, which consisted of one part of silver to two of copper. In the *Soken Kisho* three varieties of shibuichi are enumerated, — the first containing one part (by weight) of silver to three of copper; the second, one part of silver to two of copper; and the third, six or seven parts of silver to ten of copper. Concerning the third variety the author says: —"This is the best quality of shibuichi". It was always used by *Somin, Soyo,* and other great masters as a ground metal. *Soyo,* however, employed a kind of shibuichi having a dark hue, obtained apparently by an admixture of shakudo, though the compounding of these two alloys presents serious technical difficulties, and it is not known how he overcame them. Speaking generally, a greyish patina and silvery lustre are regarded as the most attractive features of shibuichi, but *Soyo*'s compound presents even choicer qualities. In the course of years the finest kind of shibuichi develops a peculiar lustrous dappling, like the marking of a tiger's skin or the ground of aventurine (nashi-ji) lacquer.

It is unnecessary to reproduce here any analytical table of shibuichi. If to what has been already said the fact be added that it contains a small quantity of gold — from 0.08 to 0.12 per cent — its composition is sufficiently described.

Mr. Gowland says of shibuichi: — The value of this alloy in decorative metal work is, like that of shakudo, entirely dependent on its patina. It possesses no special beauty when cast, its colour being that of pale gun-metal, or a common pale bronze; but when its surface is subjected to appropriate treatment, it assumes a patina of charming shades of grey, which gives it an unique position among art alloys. No other affords the artist such a delicate, unobtrusive, and effective ground for inlaid designs of gold, silver, or other metals. It was not known to the Japanese in mediaeval times. In fact, it does not appear to have been used until much later than shakudo. The descriptions given of the ornamental appendages of historical swords even as late as the seventeenth century do not mention it, and the first record we have of the alloy only dates from the beginning of the eighteenth century (1706 a.d.), when it was used in the Government Mint for the preparation of debased silver bars, termed chogin (trade silver), which were used for commercial purposes. There are several examples of its use in sword-guards about the same date, but it seems then to have been chiefly employed as a substitute for a richer alloy, a pure silver surface having been given to it by the process already described, and not the fine grey patina of later times. The patina is produced by precisely the same operations which are practised for shakudo, the solution in which the objects are boiled having the same composition as that used for the arsenical bronze, with the addition of 1 cc. of plum-vinegar to each litre. The finest grey tints are obtained only with alloys containing from 20 to 50 percent of silver. By the use in his design of both these classes of alloys, — shakudo and shibuicbi, — together with gold, silver, copper, and iron, the Japanese craftsman has achieved results in colour which are unrivalled in the metal work of the world. The white of silver, the black of shakudo, the yellows of golds of various grades, the greys of shibuicbi, and the reds and browns of copper, — all hc cmploys in harmonious combinations to enrich the effect of his sculptured work, and shows himself in all to be a true master in the art of metal decoration.

Copper was largely used in the manufacture of sword-mountings. In fact the earliest sword-guards found in Japan were made of copper thinly plated with gold. Not until a comparatively recent date, however, — probably the seventeenth century, — did Japanese artists discover and put into successful practice the patina-producing methods which impart such beauty to their work in copper, and enable them to combine it so admirably with other metals for decorative purposes. They obtain copper surfaces showing not merely a rich golden sheen with charming limpidity, but also red of various hues, from deep coral to light vermilion, several shades of grey, and brown of numerous tones, from dead-leaf to chocolate. Until the days of the Goto masters iron was the metal exclusively used for manufacturing sword-mounts, but *Goto Yujo*'s fine chiselling of shakudo, and the beautiful nanako ground that he devised for kogai and kozuka of that compound, gave it a vogue which continued uninterrupted down to modern times. Naturally a sculptor who contemplated the expenditure of much labour and skill on a small object like a guard or a dagger-haft, was careful to use iron of the highest quality only, and to anneal it by processes of which each great artist made a specialty. But no less attention was bestowed on the production of patina. The guards of early experts — the Miyochin masters down to *Nobuiye*, and the Umetada prior to *Muneyuki* — show a curious patina called moyashi, which suggests the effect that would be produced by boiling a superficial film of the metal. But from the seventeenth century onwards, the patina changes, and the surface of the metal shows a fine satin-like texture constituting one of the most beautiful features of the object. It is, indeed, a matter of constant wonder to the un-initiated that such a surface could have been imparted to iron, and the patina-producing recipes — "rust-summoning processes" (sabi-dashikata), as the Japanese call them — of the great experts would have much interest were they accessible. But these things were among the hiden, or "secret traditions," of each family of artists. No public record of them exists. Modern experts, however, though they no longer chisel sword-mounts, treat iron for artistic purposes in a manner which is at least equal to that of the old masters, and the patina-producing process for which they claim the finest results may be described here.

The first step is to obtain a mixture of finely sifted clays, red and black, which is placed in an open vessel and exposed to the action of the elements for a space of two or three years. Blue vitriol and sulphur, having then been heated together, are added to a portion of this seasoned earth, and the compound forms a paste, which is applied to the surface of the metal, this process being repeated time after time, at intervals of from four to five days, and occupying altogether about two months. If the expert judges that a good patina has been obtained, he now washes the metal carefully and polishes it with a brush (tawasbi) of rice-straw. This preliminary polishing is a long business, and when it has been carried far enough, the final burnishing is done with dried spikelets of the pine-tree, after which it remains only to damp the object repeatedly with an infusion of tea-leaves during four or five days. Such is the method pursued by Ito Katsumi, a modern expert of the highest skill. Another plan, more curious and said to be very efficacious, is to substitute for the mixture of red and black earth mentioned above some charcoal ashes taken from beneath the gridiron on which eels have been roasted. Into an open vessel containing this ash a small bag of sulphur is inserted, and the mixture is exposed in the open air for two or three years, by which time the ash has become thoroughly impregnated with sulphur. Repeated coats of it are then applied to the iron object at intervals, for about two months, after which polishing and burnishing are effected as before. Tradition says that the early Miyochin masters burnished their iron with a cotton cloth dipped in the juice of the lacquer-tree, but there is no certainty as to that point.

It is understood, of course, that the processes here described are peculiar to certain experts. Many quaint recipes might be obtained by setting down the alleged hiden of this family or that. But it is plain that the published accounts of these methods are intended to deceive rather than to instruct. Scarcely less important in Japanese eyes than the chiselling of the decorative design itself is the preparation of the field to which it is applied. This part of the subject has hitherto received little attention from European and American commentators, possibly because it has a technical rather than an artistic character.

The translation given above from the *Soken Kisho* shows that nanako (fish-roe grounds) were counted de-rigueur for kogai or kozuka from the time (1469) of *Goto Yujo*, and that grounds in the ishime (stone-pitting) or jimigaki (polished) style were not considered proper for swords worn on ceremonial occasions. These remarks do not apply to iron sword-mounts. In the case of iron the patina alone was esteemed. Sometimes, though very rarely, the coarsest kind of ishime (arashi-ishime) was employed even on iron guards to heighten the effect of recessed chiselling, but it is generally true that shakudo was the favourite metal for nanako grounds, and shibuichi or copper for ishime. As a broad definition it may be said that nanako is obtained by punching the whole surface, except the portion carrying the decorative design, into a texture of microscopic dots. The first makers of nanako did not aim at regularity in the distribution of these dots: they were content to produce the effect of millet-seed sifted, haphazard, over the surface. But very soon —certainly by the time of *Goto Yujo* — the punching of the dots in rigidly straight lines came to be considered essential, and the difficulty involved in this tour de force was so great that nanako making took its place among the highest technical achievements of the sculptor. When it is remembered that the punching-tool was guided solely by the hand and eye, and that three or more blows of the mallet had to be struck for every dot, some idea may be formed of the patience and accuracy needed to produce these tiny protuberances in perfectly straight lines at exactly equal intervals and of absolutely uniform size, so that a magnifying-glass can scarcely detect any variation in their order or size. Nanako disposed in straight parallel lines has always ranked at the head of this kind of work, but a new style was introduced in 1560 by *Matabei*, the second representative of the Muneta family. It was obtained by punching the dots in intersecting lines, so arranged that the dots fell uniformly into diamond-shaped groups of five each. This is called go-no-me (some-times gu-no-me) nanako, because of its resemblance to the disposition of chequers in the Japanese game of go. A century later (1640), another representative of the Muneta family — *Norinao*, known in the art world as *Doki* — invented a new style of nanako to which the name of daimyo-nanako was given, doubtless because its special excellence seemed to reserve it for the use of the great nobles (daimyo) only.

In this variety the lines of dots alternated with lines of polished ground. Ishime may be described briefly as diapering. A diapered ground is known in Japan, however, by the special term wari-ishime (i.e. ishime distributed in patterns). There is scarcely any limit to the ingenuity and skill of the Japanese expert in diapering a metal surface. Thus one may see a silver teapot having its surface recessed in forty or fifty leaf-shaped panels, each panel filled with a different diaper of minute and delicate workmanship. But the ishime used on the fields of sword-mounts does not belong to the diaper class, according to Japanese nomenclature. There are, first, the zara-maki (broad-cast), — sometimes called tatsuta-maki, — in which the surface is finely but irregularly pitted, after the manner of the face of a stone; second, the kashiji (pear-ground) ishime, which gives a surface like the rind of a pear; third, the hari-ishime, where the indentations are so minute that they seem to have been made with the point of a needle (hart); fourth, the gama-ishime, which is intended to imitate the skin of a toad (gama); fifth, the tsuya-ishime (lustrous), produced with a chisel sharpened so that its traces have a brilliant appearance; sixth, orekuchi (broken-tool) ishime, a peculiar kind obtained by fracturing a chisel and hammering the surface of the metal with the jagged tool (this last variety is spoken of as arashi-ishime, a generic term applied to all rough work); and seventh, gozame-ishime, so called because it resembles the plaited surface of a fine straw-mat. These details may seem insignificant, but without some knowledge of them it is impossible to appreciate the quality of Japanese metal work. A word must also be said about the different methods of chiselling. Of these the most important is taka-bori, or chiselling in relief. The Japanese distinguish three varieties of relief carving, namely, atsu-niku-bori (high relief), or alto relievo; chiu-niku-bori (medium relief), mezzo relievo; usu-niku-bori (low relief) or basso relievo. These expressions explain themselves. But it may be added that, in the opinion of the Japanese expert, they occupy the same respective rank as the three kinds of ideographic script occupy in the realm of calligraphy. High-relief carving corresponds with the kai-sho, or most correct and classical form of writing; medium relief, with the gyo-sho, or semi-cursive style; and low-relief, with the so-sho or grass character. Passing to incised chiselling, the commonest form is ke-bori, or "hair cutting," which may be called engraving, the lines being of uniform thickness and depth. Very beautiful results are obtained by the ke-bori (kebori) method. But incomparably the finest work in the incised class is that known as kata-kiri-bori. In this kind of chiselling the Japanese expert claims to be unique as well as unrivalled. It is easy to see that the idea of the great Yokoya experts, the originators of this style, was to break away from the somewhat formal monotony of ordinary engraving, where each line performs exactly the same function, and to convert the chisel into an artist's brush instead of using it as a common cutting-tool. They succeeded admirably. In the kata-kiri-bori every line has its proper value in the pictorial design, and strength and directness become prime elements in the strokes of the burin, just as they do in the brush-work of the picture-painter. It may be said, indeed, that the same fundamental rule applied whether the field of the decoration was silk, paper, or metal: the artist's tool, be it brush or burin, had to perform its task by one effort. There must be no appearance of subsequent deepening, or extending, or re-cutting, or finishing. Kata-kiri-bori by a great expert is a delight. One is lost in astonishment at the nervous yet perfectly regulated force and the unerring fidelity of every trace of the chisel. Low-relief chiselling does not easily lend itself to the production of striking effects, but the skill exhibited by many Japanese experts in this kind of work was even more remarkable than that of its great Italian master *Donatello*, and when combined with kata-kiri chiselling it gave exquisite pictures. Another variety much affected by artists of the seventeenth century and subsequent eras was called shishi-ai-bori, or niku-ai-bori. In this the surface of the design was not raised above the general plane of the field, but an effect of projection was obtained by recessing the whole space immediately surrounding the design or by enclosing the latter in a scarped frame. Again, in many sword-guards the design was modelled on both faces so as to be a complete sculpture. This fashion was always accompanied by chiselling à jour (sukashi-bori), so that the sculptured portions stood out in their entirety. All fully modelled work, whether for guards, menuki, or other purposes, was called maru-bori (round carving). Inlaying with gold or silver was among the early forms of decoration. There were two principal kinds of inlaying: the first called hon-zogan (true inlaying);

the second nunome-zogan (linen-mesh inlaying). As to the former, the Japanese method did not differ from that seen in the beautiful iron censers and vases inlaid with gold which the Chinese produced with notable success from the Shun-tieh era (1426—1436).

In the surface of the metal the workman cut grooves wider at the base than at the top, and then hammered into them gold or silver wire. Such a process presents no remarkable features, except that it has been carried by Japanese experts to an extraordinary degree of elaboration. The nunome-zogan is much more interesting. Suppose, for example, that the artist desires to produce an inlaid diaper. His first business is to chisel the surface in lines forming the basic pattern of the design. Thus, for a diamond petal diaper the chisel is carried across the face of the metal horizontally, tracing a number of parallel bands, divided at fixed intervals by ribs, which are obtained by merely straightening the chisel and striking it a heavy blow. The same process is then repeated in another direction, so that the new bands cross the old at an angle adapted to the nature of the design. Several independent chisellings may be necessary before the lines of the diaper emerge clearly, but throughout the whole operation no measurement of any kind is taken: the artist is guided entirely by his eye, though the slightest failure to estimate the dimensions correctly, or the slightest deviation of hand or chisel would at once destroy the work. The metal is then heated, not to redness, but sufficiently to develop a certain degree of softness, and the workman, taking a very thin sheet of gold, hammers portions of it into the salient points of the design, thus clearly marking out the spaces. In ordinary cases this is the sixth process. The seventh is to hammer gold into the outlines of the diaper; the eighth, to hammer it into the pattern filling the spaces between the lines, and the ninth and tenth to complete the details of the pattern. Of course the more intricate the design the more numerous the processes. The expert uses magnifying-glasses, but is said to depend more on the delicacy of his own sense of touch than on the power of the glasses. It is scarcely possible to imagine a higher effort of hand and eye than this nunome-zogan displays, for while intricacy and elaborateness are carried to the very extreme, absolutely mechanical accuracy is obtained. Sometimes into the same design gold enters in three different hues, obtained by varying the alloy.

A third kind of inlaying, peculiar to Japan, is sumi-zogan (ink inlaying), so called because the inlaid design gives the impression of having been painted with Indian ink beneath the transparent surface of the metal. The difference between this process and ordinary inlaying is that for sumi-zogan the design to be inlaid is fully chiselled out of an independent block of metal, with sides sloping so as to be broader at the base than at the top. The object which is to receive the decoration is then channelled in dimensions corresponding with those of the design-block, and the latter having been fixed in the channel, the surface is ground and polished until absolute intimacy seems to be obtained between the inlaid design and the metal forming its field. Very beautiful effects are thus produced, for the design seems to have grown up to the surface of the metal field rather than to have been planted in it. Shibuichi inlaid with shakudo used to be the commonest combination of metals in this class of decoration, and the objects usually depicted were bamboos, crows, wild-fowl under the moon, peony sprays, and so forth. It remains to refer to a variety of decoration specially affected by the early experts and subsequently carried to a high degree of excellence, namely, mokume-ji, or wood-grained ground. The process in this case is to take a thin plate of iron — if iron is to be treated — and beat into it another plate of similar metal, so that the two, though welded together, retain their separate forms. The mass, while still hot, is coated with hena-tsuchi (a kind of gray clay) and rolled in straw ash, in which state it is roasted over a charcoal fire raised to glowing heat with the bellows. The clay having been removed, another plate of metal is beaten in, and the same process is repeated. This is done several times, the number depending on the quality of graining that the expert desires to produce. The manifold plate is then heavily punched from one side so that the opposite face protrudes in broken blisters, which are then hammered down until each becomes a centre of wave propagation. In fine work the apex of the blister is ground off before the final hammering. It will be evident that the wood-graining is obtained on one face of the metal only by this process. Hence, when there is question of a sword-guard, two plates have to be separately prepared, and afterwards welded together, back to back. Iron was used exclusively for work of this kind down to the sixteenth century, but various metals began to be thenceforth combined. Perhaps the choicest variety is gold graining in a shakudo field. By repeated hammering and polishing the expert obtains such control of the wood-grain pattern that its sinuosities and eddies seem to have developed symmetry without losing anything of their fantastic grace. Another method of producing mokume-ji was to take the plate, — composed of various laminae as described above, — set it on its edge and hammer it so that it spread in a direction perpendicular to its original face. The new plate was then fixed on a different edge and once more hammered flat. By these devices graining with elongated curves was produced. Sometimes the expert, having welded together the several sheets of metal, fixed the plate on edge at an angle more or less acute, and beat it out by a series of blows which had the effect of peeling the surface and re-distributing it in a kind of wave diaper. Such work demanded much skill and care. The rings and caps of hilts were often decorated in the mokume style. In these cases the plate of grained metal was bent to the required shape and veneered to a base of thicker metal. The metal-workers of Nagoya, from the middle of the eighteenth century, produced excellent mokume grounds. Their favourite plan was to weld four or five lamina of different metals — iron, shakudo, copper, shibuichi, silver and sometimes gold — into a sheet. The corners of the latter were then cut off, and the plate, having been reheated, was placed vertically on each of the four sections in succession, and beaten flat by strokes delivered from the opposite section. These Nagoya experts were also successful with a special kind of mokume known as tama-mokume. The different metals, having been reduced to spherical form, are loaded like bullets into an iron cylinder, which is brought to a red heat, placed vertically on the anvil and hammered into a plate. In this kind of mokume the contours of the graining take a circular form. One other variety of decoration has to be mentioned. It is called gun-son, and its model is taken from the well-known tsui-shiu (or tsui-koku) lacquer, which shows a formal diaper cut deeply into several coats of superposed lacquer, the channels being narrower below than above, so that the slope of their sides enables the various strata of the lacquer coats to be clearly seen. To produce this effect in metal, alternating plates of two metals, or perhaps three, were welded together, and when they had been shaped into the form of the object projected, the design was deeply chiselled, the channels ultimately presenting horizontally streaked sides. The guri-bori exhibits technical skill only, but it is worth noting that although in nearly all the processes of decorative metal work modern Japanese experts are at least as skilled as their predecessors, they fail to produce this particular kind successfully. The experts of former times seem to have possessed some secret for welding together their sheets of metal so that each sheet preserved its individuality though intimately joined to its companions above and below. Experts of the present day are compelled to resort to solder, and it is evident that to lay solder in an absolutely even coat over the surface of a metal plate is almost impossible. Somewhere there is a break of continuity, and a flaw results when the pile of plates is channelled.

It is certainly a close approximation to the truth to say that before the time of *Yujo*, the first of the Goto masters, — that is to say, before the year 1469, when he began to develop the style for which he afterwards became so famous, — chiselling in relief was not applied to the decoration of sword-ornaments in such a manner as to command public admiration. Some investigators carry the statement still farther: they allege that *Goto Yujo* actually invented relief carving. Possibly the assertion is true if it is understood in the sense of relief without the aid of the repoussé process. Decoration in relief had been applied to armour by the Miyochin masters for certainly three centuries, and perhaps four, before *Yujo*'s era. But lightness being of prime importance in the case of armour, the artist naturally had recourse to the repoussé method for the raised parts of the decorative design, and though he used his chisel for finishing off the work, he never attempted to cut the design out of the solid metal. It was left to *Goto Yujo* to develop the potentialities of that method.

An element of confusion has been introduced into this chapter of history by writers who represent the celebrated *Kaneiye* as having chiselled sword-guards with designs in relief before the time of *Yujo*. M. *Louis Gonse*, for example, says that *Kaneiye* worked at the close of the fourteenth century, and describes guards by him which show that chiselling in relief was then practised. *Kaneiye* certainly did employ the method of relief chiselling in manufacturing guards. He worked, however, not at the end of the fourteenth century, but at the beginning of the sixteenth.

There is, indeed, a little uncertainty about his date. Some records call him a pupil of *Nobuiye*, which would place him about the year 1520; others assign him to a slightly earlier epoch. At all events *Goto Yujo* had been working for at least twenty or thirty years before *Kaneiye's* time, and the true historical relation in which the two men stand to each other is that *Yujo* invented relief chiselling and *Kaneiye* was the first to apply it to sword-guards. For *Goto Yujo* was not a guard-maker. He never chiselled a guard, but devoted his attention solely to the smaller mounts, namely, the menuki, the kogai, and the kozuka. It has been stated by European writers that from the artistic stand-point the guard is the most important part of the sword's furniture. That view would not be admitted by any Japanese connoisseur. In Japan, from the time when glyptic artists began to occupy themselves with the decoration of sword-mounts, a clear distinction was always drawn between the essential and the ornamental parts. The former comprised the guard, the ring, and the crown [fuchi and kashira] of the hilt; the latter, the menuki, the kogai, and the kozuka. Until the seventeenth century the three last were known as the kit-su-dokoro (three parts), and though the distinction ceased to be rigid in later times, it was carefully observed by the early Goto masters as well as by their contemporaries, and every connoisseur knows that on the mitsu-dokoro are to be found the most delicate workmanship and the most elaborate decorative effects in the whole range of Japanese metal work. The guard has special attractions which cannot be imparted to such comparatively petty objects as the kogai or the kozuka, but it is not to the guard alone or chiefly that the student must look for the history of this branch of Japanese art. *Goto Yujo's* skill was expended almost solely on the menuki and the kogai. So far as concerns the menuki, he cannot be credited with much originality. During certainly two, and probably seven, centuries before his time, the menuki had received attention at the hands of glyptic experts, and had been variously decorated according to the fancy of the swordsman or the genius of the artist. *Yujo* merely brought to the chiselling of these little objects a new quality of skill, and to the designing of their forms, in his later years, a new wealth of fancy derived from the co-operation of the renowned pictorial artist *Kano Masanobu*. Besides, although the beauty of the menuki was incalculably increased by *Yujo*, he made no radical change in the method of chiselling it. In his hands it remained what it had been in the hands of his predecessors, either repoussé work with fine surface chiselling, or, in rare cases, a solid carving. It has been argued that since the kozuka and the kogai had a place in the scabbard of the wakizashi for at least two centuries before Goto's time, and since such unrivalled armourers as the Miyochin no Judai (the Ten Miyochin generations) as well as two of the Six Giyoshi, were his predecessors, the ornamentation of these portions of the sword-furniture must have occupied the hands of experts prior to the fifteenth century. Critics holding that view would place *Yujo* at the apex of an art movement rather than regard him as its originator, and would derive his great reputation from his excellence rather than from his originality. It must be admitted that such a theory is not inconsistent with facts which confront the student in other developments of Japanese art. However, the sum of accessible knowledge seems to be that never until *Yujo* began to work did the art of chiselling in relief become a really admirable accomplishment. Concerning the question whether *Yujo* was a great expert, the answer given by many foreign connoisseurs is negative. While granting that he stood at the head of a school, they allege that it was the classical school; in other words, a school which did not conceive the possibility, or perhaps admit the propriety, of aiming at such qualities as softness, delicacy, and pictorial ideality in the decoration of metallic surfaces, especially when the object to be decorated formed part of a weapon of war. Some even go so far as to assert that the severe formality and narrow range of the early Goto experts are as far removed from the graceful tenderness and wide repertoire of the eighteenth-century artists — the *Hamano* and the *Ishiguro*, for example — as are the three chisels of *Ichikawa Hirosuke* from the three hundred of *Kashiwaya Nagatsune*. Now it is quite true that *Yujo* conceived the dragon and the Dog of Fo (shishi) to be the most appropriate objects for representation on arms and armour. The dragon pre-eminently occupied his attention. He devoted infinite care to the modelling of every part of the monster, and elaborated for himself exact. rules as to the shape and dimensions of the claws, the horns, the scales, the teeth, the ears, and the armature. There are points here which probably lie beyond the appreciation of a foreign connoisseur, who regards the dragon as on the whole an ugly reptile, and can scarcely accept it as an agreeable element of any decorative scheme. But to a Japanese artist or lover of art the dragon, with its fierce vitality and mysterious suggestions, is a creature of the highest interest. The painter and the sculptor alike understood the immense difficulty of depicting or chiselling it so that it should have the semblance of ferocious vigour and implacable malignity, not the appearance of a limp, fantastic worm. All the Goto masters made a close study of the dragon. They showed it in various shapes and positions, and in chiselling it they acquired certain mannerisms from which skilled connoisseurs in later ages constructed an alphabet of identification. Thus, at the beginning of the eighteenth century, there was published a two-volume book (Kinko Kantei Hiketsu, or the secrets of judging works in gold), containing minute analyses of what are known as the hiden (secret formulas) of the first fifteen Goto masters. It is a compilation of interest, as showing the lovingly appreciative attention bestowed upon such objects by Japanese connoisseurs. But almost everything is based upon the dragon, and certainly an exceptional instinct is required for undertaking a careful study of that fabulous and repellent monster, from the contours of his curves and the angles of his claws to the length of his antennas, the set of his ears, and the section of his horns. If an estimate of the Goto family's work were derived from the contents of that brochure alone, it would be necessary to endorse the verdict which accuses them of classical severity and narrow range of motive. But there is other and more trustworthy evidence — the Manpo Zensho (complete treatise on all precious things), published in 1711, as well as a manuscript handed down through six generations of a family whose successive representatives were professional connoisseurs of sword-blades and sword-furniture. It will be worth while to quote from these compilations some of the information furnished about the works of the first six Goto masters, because not only is an insight thus obtained into Japanese views about these products of art, but also much is learned about the decorative motives chosen by these six experts between the years 1460 and 1631: —

1. Among authenticated specimens of the first six *Goto* masters, there are not any that have a copper ground with trees, reeds, shrubs, or flowers chiselled in relief.

2. Specimens decorated with various kinds of crustacea, or with landscapes in which living creatures do not appear, are considered of inferior quality. The same remark applies to *kogai* and *menuki* chiselled with scattered-leaf designs only.

3. Each stroke of the chisel must be clean and even, showing everywhere strength and directness.

4. With regard to the objeets depicted, it is essential to observe that the faces of human beings must faithfully reflect the sentiments supposed to animate them. Under painful circumstances the faces portrayed by the Goto masters are always distressed; in joyful conditions, they are merry. Such is seldom the case in the works of the carvers of the branch houses (Waki-bori), or of men that make a commerce of their art (Machi-bori, or street-carvers, and Inari-bori, a term of uncertain origin). The Goto oxen are always sleek and fairly proportioned, not the gaunt, bony animals of lesser experts. Their horses are full-girthed, strong, and spirited. Their crows, even the blackest, have a peculiar light-hued mark at the stem of the feathers, and their white herons a gold point under the eye. The chiselling of the dragons' faces constitutes a special distinction, and the same remark applies to the Kara-shishi (Dog of Fo). Water from which a dragon emerges is always rough and has many wave-crests, but water above which the ama-ryo flies has few crests; and water over which the moon shines is calm, with only occasional ripples. The carp also springs from quiet water, and where flower-rafts are shown floating on a lake or river, the whole scene, from the placid water to the softly contoured rocks, is restful and smiling. Association of blossom-boats with beetling cliffs, angry waves, and swirling currents, is the false conception of a bad artist. Flowers and shrubs, however, do not appear much on the works of the Goto masters, or, if they appear, belong to a comparatively low grade of chiselling. Still there is a fine specimen of *Yujo's* work that forms an exception to this rule. It is a kogai of shakudo, having a single chrysanthemum carved in relief, and a tanzaku (tablet) on which the following couplet is inlaid with gold: —

"Until the dew flake,
Beading this blossom's gold,
Swells to a broad lake,
Age after age untold
Joy to joy manifold
Add for thy sweet sake."

Other exceptions are the following specimens, which, if the great masters' works be divided in three classes with three grades in each class, must stand in the first grade of the second class,

(1) A kogai by *Yujo*, on which the design is a rain-pipe with a wistaria clasping it. The chiselling is in high relief, the creeper and the pipe are plated with gold, and the other parts are in shakudo.

(2) A kozuka of shakudo by *Yujo*, having for design a tuft of susuki (Eularia Japonica) in silver and gold under a shibuichi moon. The scene represents the Moor of Musashi.

(3) A kogai of shakudo by *Yujo*, on which the design is a bamboo water-pipe, having beside it eight Kiri (Paulownia) blossoms within a circle. An idea of the extreme delicacy of *Yujo*'s chiselling may be formed from a celebrated work of his, a peach-kernel upon which he carved the twenty-one Shrines of Sanno, standing among trees peopled by a multitude of monkeys. A favourite form of menuki chiselled by the Goto masters was a dragon coiled round a two-edged sword (called kuri-kara-ryu). In good specimens of these menuki the sword passes perfectly straight through the coils of the dragon, and the blade flashes. The slightest deviation from the straight line is a blemish. Many other specimens are mentioned, — the Dragon King riding on a carp; a tenniu reading a sutra; fishing with cormorants at Nagara; Asaina and the demon trying their strength; fishing by flash-light; a child catching a crab; Fukurokuju feeding his crane; Kengiu and Shokujo; Choryo and Sekiko; *Nō* dancers; long-armed apes clutching at the moon's reflection; lobsters; insects of various kinds; a rat trapped by a clam; cats catching rats; rats eating mochi; puppy dogs playing with empty shells or holding fans in their teeth; a child setting a dog at a blind man; bulls fighting; oxen ploughing; flower-rafts floating down rivers; carp leaping up water-falls; various scenes from the twenty-four acts of filial piety, and so on.

In short, these records show that the first six Goto masters had a very large repertoire of subjects, and that it is altogether a mistake to speak of their productions as severely classical, or of their range of decorative motives as limited. They differed, of course, in the quality of their work, the third representative, *Joshiu*, being notably the coarsest and roughest chiseller among them. It is a theory implicitly believed in Japan that an artist's moral nature is reflected in his productions. *Joshiu* was a big, stalwart soldier. He fell in battle, the end he had always desired, and there is certainly something of the bluff man-at-arms in his style of carving. His most elaborate effort is said to have been a pair of menuki in the form of a procession of golden ants carrying silver eggs. But he preferred fierce dragons and angry *shishi*. His son *Kwojo*, the fourth representative, who worked from 1550 to 1620, is distinguished for precisely the quality which his father lacked, extreme accuracy of detail and delicacy of style. Up to *Kwojo*'s time, that is to say, during the era of the first three Goto masters, the iroye (literally, colour-picture) process, or "picking out" with metal different from that of the general design, was somewhat clumsy. The preparation of efficient solder not being understood, the expert had to pin each tiny plate of gold, silver, or copper in its place. He accomplished this with such dexterity that the rivets were not visible, but really delicate work could not be done. In Kwojo's time a solder was discovered so good that a piece of metal fixed with it could be afterwards chiselled in loco. The use of this '*ro*' (literally, wax), as the Japanese called it, made an immense difference in the quality of detail chiselling, and the uttori iroye (riveted plating) of the first Goto experts was finally abandoned. It is unnecessary to enter into any further analysis of the Goto masters' work. What has been said above of the first six generations applies to the methods of all their successors. The influence exercised by the family and its branches in this particular sphere of Japanese art was enormous. Until the time of *Kwojo* and *Tokujo* sword-mounts were valued solely for their uses: the idea of collecting and treasuring them as objects of art does not appear to have occurred to any dilettante. But when the reign of peace inaugurated by the Tokugawa regents gave people leisure to think of the sword's furniture as much as of its blade, it began to be the fashion to make collections of the beautiful specimens of sculpture in metal, then produced in large quantities in the capitals of many of the fifes; and from that era until the present, it was always considered that the basis of every good collection must be a series representing the works of the first fourteen Goto experts, from *Yujo* to *Keijo*. Any careful student of the subject who has had an opportunity of examining the splendid works of other great masters, will be disposed to rebel against the factitious prominence thus assigned to the productions of the Goto, — the iye-bori, or "carvings of the family," as they are called. Yet the Japanese verdict is probably correct, for the foundation of this branch of art is undoubtedly relief-chiselling, and whether the Goto masters originated that style or merely raised it from a condition of tentative inferiority to a state of the highest perfection, the credit belongs to them of having demonstrated its capabilities, and thus opened to Japanese sculptors a path leading to results absolutely unrivalled in the corresponding work, of other nations. It is worth while to note here that at the beginning of the present century (20th) a kogai a kozuka or a pair of menuki authenticated as fine specimens of an early Goto master, commanded a price of from £8 to £40. Recapitulating the art relations of the Goto's work, the broad facts are that they introduced the style of carving in relief without the aid of repoussé; that they invented, or, at all events, raised to an admirable grade, the nanako grounds which form such beautiful fields for metal sculpture of every kind; that they devised the method of "picking out," or plating with various metals in order to produce pictorial effects; and that they carried the process of gold inlaying to a point of delicacy far beyond the conception of previous artists. It is curious that this last development should stand chiefly to the credit of the third representative, *Joshiu*, otherwise a comparatively rough expert. Not until the time of *Tokujo*, the fifth of the Goto masters, who worked from 1561 to 1631, is there any evidence that guards or fuchi-gashira were among the productions of the family, and, on the whole, their work in that particular line may be dismissed as inappreciable. In fact, guard-making remained for a long time the special business of the armourer, and the method of decoration adopted was either to impart to the outline of the guard some quaint shape, or to weld it in such a manner that the surface presented the appearance of wood graining, or to decorate it with designs chiselled à jour.

As to the first method, nothing need be said: it was a device within the range of the most ordinary skill. But the wood-grain (mokume) surface must be classed among the remarkable achievements of the Japanese armourer. It seems impossible to determine when this curious tour-de-force had its origin. The oldest examples of it spoken of by Japanese connoisseurs are from the hands of Miyochin Munesuke, who worked from 1154 to 1185 a.d. Munesuke is generally regarded as the founder of the great Miyochin family of armourers. He was, in fact, the twentieth representative, the founder having been *Munemichi*, who flourished in the seventh century. But *Munesuke* stands so far above all his predecessors that he justly deserves to be called the father of Japanese armourers. He is the first of the yudai, or ten great generations of Miyochin experts, ending with *Muneyasu* in 1380. It was he that forged *Yoshitsune*'s magnificent suit of armour. Many of his iron guards are fine examples of the mokume-ji, or wood-grain forging which has already been described. *Munesuke* marked these guards Shinto go-tetsu-ren, or "five-times-forged iron of the sacred way," and it may here be added that, in common with the great experts of his family, the ideographs used in his inscriptions for guards are of the kind called kabuto-ji or "helmet characters;" that is to say, the grass script (sosho) with curled strokes; an ornamental style of writing always employed in marking helmets. From the time of *Munesuke* down to the present era the production of wood-grain effects has been among the remarkable achievements of Japanese workers. The Miyochin master used iron only. As to guards having designs chiselled à jour {sukashi-bori}, it is generally believed that up to the close of the fifteenth century they were more or less roughly executed. Some connoisseurs claim that *Miyochin Nobuiye*, who worked during the early part of the sixteenth century, was the first to carry this method of decoration to a point of really high excellence. *Nobuiye* was third of the Nochi no San-saku, or "Three Later Masters," of the Miyochin family, and it is scarcely credible that his two immediate predecessors, *Yoshimichi* (1530) and *Takayoshi* (1490), the other two of the renowned trio, who worked during the epoch when the Goto family's skill had given new importance to the decoration of sword-mounts, can have failed to produce fine guards in the sukashi style.

Indeed many delicately chiselled and artistically conceived guards exist in Japan which are attributed, with apparent reason, to makers of earlier eras than *Nobuiye*'s. But the question need not be discussed here. *Nobuiye* himself did not generally approve of weakening a guard by pierced carving of such an elaborate character as was subsequently adopted, nor must his methods be inferred from the numerous specimens bearing his name, since, in the first place, many of them are forgeries by makers of later epochs, and, in the second, two other experts of the same name — one of *Aki*, the other of *Kishiu* — manufactured guards some of which have been confounded with the work of the Miyochin master. In *Nobuiye*'s finest guards there are found two styles: first, line engraving combined with chiselling in very low relief; and secondly, decoration à jour. Guards of the former class have the surface covered with an engraved floral scroll (karakusa), among which are leaves and blossoms (generally of the Paulownia or the evening gourd) in slight relief. These works plainly show the influence which the Goto family's methods had already exercised upon the fashion of the time. In the guards with pierced decoration, the commonest designs are a network pattern [*ami-gata*] or a kikko diaper (tortoise-shell tessellation), and occasionally verses of poetry occur, the ideographs cut right through the metal so accurately and delicately that each character seems to be written by a skilled penman with white ink on the russet patina of the iron. Among specimens of *Nobuiye*'s guards preserved in Japan, the sacrifice of solidity to decorative design is carried farthest in one which has in the centre a torii (sacred bird-perch) within a frame of mokko-gata (four-arched outline). The torii alone is solid, all the remaining space within the frame being cut out. Another remarkable guard by the same maker, which the inscription shows to have been forged for the notorious Anayama, has the surface covered with deep pitting, the depressions and elevations alternating on the two faces. All the guards of the Miyochin experts, from *Munesuke* to *Nobuiye*, are slightly rough to the touch, though they present the appearance of finely finished work. This peculiarity — called by the Japanese moyashi, or fermentation — is the result of the patina-producing process. It need scarcely be said that the patina was a point of the greatest importance. The most prized variety had the colour of the azuki bean, or dark mahogany.

The chisellers of guards with decoration à jour showed a fertile fancy in choosing and inventing designs. Naturally their work was not uniformly good. The great majority of the inferior samurai and all the common foot-soldiers [*ashigaru*] had to be content with weapons on which little decorative labour had been expended. But with the nobles and the officers of rank the case was different. At their order the great armourers, and subsequently the chisellers of sword-mounts, worked with ever-increasing rivalry to produce fine guards which, while presenting an appearance of lightness and delicacy, nevertheless possessed all the elements of strength and durability necessary in a soldier's weapons. Many of these guards are interesting and valuable for the sake of the decorative ability and extraordinary technical skill that they display; but they belong, of course, to a class of artistic workmanship distinct from that of the surface-chiselled sword-mounts of later times. It may be well here to dismiss, once for all, a theory sometimes advanced by writers in Europe that many of the elaborate guards of the fifteenth and sixteenth centuries were of cast iron. That cast-iron guards had no existence cannot be affirmed; they may sometimes have been made for weapons of the most inferior description. But the Japanese themselves deny that cast iron was ever regarded as a suitable material for a sword-guard, its liability to fracture being a fatal objection. The connoisseur — and every samurai was something of a connoisseur in matters concerning his sword— attached more importance to the tempering of the metal than to the fashion of the ornamental chiselling, and in every record of great armourers skill in forging iron heads the list of their achievements. There is a story told of a celebrated swordsman of Owari, *Yagiu* by name, who in the sixteenth century had fifty fine sword-guards made by the best experts of the time. He placed all the guards in a mortar, pounded them with a heavy pestle, and used only those that survived the ordeal. Subsequently *Yagiu*'s guards came to be the fashion, and were preferred to much finer work which had not undergone the same test. There is, however, an explanation of the cast-iron theory advanced by European writers. Many of the guards sold to foreign collectors in recent times have been of cast iron, made expressly for the unwary curio hunter. From these a deceptive inference has been drawn as to the nature of the genuine old work. In describing briefly the progress of the art from the time of its early prosperity until the present day, the most convenient method will be to follow the method of division into centuries.

SIXTEENTH CENTURY

Two eminently great names of this century are *Nobuiye* (Miyochin) and *Kaneiye*, but enough has already been said about their work. It may be added here, however, that although the great *Kaneiye* certainly flourished at the close of the fifteenth and the beginning of the sixteenth century, Japanese traditions refer to an earlier expert of the same name whom they distinguish as *O-shodai Kaneiye*, or the "remote first-generation *Kaneiye*." Nothing accurate is known about him, and the few specimens attributed to him are of such inferior quality that no interest attaches to their history. Concerning the Miyochin family, it is to be noted that they did not contribute much to the decoration of sword-furniture. They were essentially armourers, though they produced also many objects which do not belong to the category of arms or armour, — for example, censers, alcove-ornaments, metal mountings for palanquins, and so forth. The list of Miyochin masters who worked in the sixteenth century includes many names, — *Katsumasa, Katsuiye, Nobuyoshi, Nobusada, Muneaki, Kunishige, Muneharu, Munenori, Munehisa,* etc., — but as makers of sword-mounts they may be dismissed with the remark that they confined themselves to chiselling iron guards with pierced decoration or with wood-grained surface. The name of one, *Miyochin Fusayoshi*, has been handed down to posterity on account of his skill in cutting chrysanthemums à jour; and *Iyefusa*, a pupil of *Nobuiye*, became celebrated for similar work. In nearly all cases where an artist achieved success as a worker in metals, a number of students flocked to his workshop, and these, together with his own sons and descendants, founded a line of experts perpetuating the family's name and its style from generation to generation.

The Goto and Miyochin houses are conspicuous examples, but scores of other families swell the list. Several had their origin, and attained special fame, in the sixteenth century. Reference has already been made to the Umetada family, whose representative, *Shigeyoshi*, became famous at the end of the fourteenth century, working for the Ashikaga Shogun, *Yoshimitsu*.

A much more highly skilled artist of the same house — also called *Shigeyoshi* (art name, *Miyoju*) — chiselled guards with decoration à jour in the middle of the sixteenth century, thus bringing the Umetada family into greater repute than ever. There was a third *Shigeyoshi* (art name, *Meishin*), who, though he flourished in the seventeenth century (1630), may be mentioned here for the sake of distinctness. This last, working for the Court in Yedo, received the honorary title of Ho-kyo, and added chiselling in relief to the à jour decoration which alone had been practised by his predecessors. Thus it may be said that the Umetada family had three epochs, — its debut upon the art stage at the beginning of the eleventh century when its then noble representative, *Tachibana no Munechika*, became the renowned swordsmith known through all time as *Sanjo no Kokaji*; its earliest remarkable connection with guard-chiselling in the days of the first *Shigeyoshi* (1400); and its attainment of high rank in that line when (1630) the third *Shigeyoshi* (*Meishin*) worked for the second Tokugawa Shogun. This somewhat tedious analysis is made because great confusion has crept into the writings of European connoisseurs in the matter of the Umetada family. The reader will understand that the family did not cease to produce skilled experts after the third Shigeyoshi, but it is impossible to find space here for detailed reference except in the case of great celebrities. The *Muneta* family, which gave to Japan another long line of experts, was founded in Kyoto in 1520 by *Matazayemon*. At first the *Muneta* masters confined themselves to working in silver, but *Matabei* (1560), grandson of *Matazayemon*, having invented the style of nanako called *go-no-me* (as already mentioned), he and his successors, down to the middle of the century, are chiefly remembered for their skill in that kind of work. *Muneta Naomichi* (1660) — art name, *Dochoku* — was the first of the family to attain great distinction for chiselling in high relief and in the *shishi-ai-bori* method (recessed carving). He and his sons, *Naoshige* and *Naomine*, worked in Osaka, and are among the most celebrated experts of that city.

The *Aoki* family came to notice in this century. Founded (1580) by *Jubei* (art name, *Tetsujin*, i.e. worker in iron), who entered the service of the feudal chief of Higo, and settled at Hasuike in that province. Jubei, spoken of as the successor of *Kaneiye*, apparently because he resembled the latter in style and was not much inferior to him in skill. He also has the credit of introducing brass into the decorative designs on iron sword-guards. But the latter specialty is more correctly associated with the name of *Jingo*, who worked at Yatsushiro, in the same province of Higo, in 1630. *Jingo*'s guards have brass decoration, boldly chiselled in very high relief. They were always greatly appreciated in Japan, though their workmanship scarcely seems to merit that distinction. *Jingo-tsuba* came to be the generic term for all guards having brass decorative designs on an iron ground. The *Soami* (*Shoami*) family was founded at the end of the fourteenth century by *Masanori*, but its work did not attract public attention until the time (1410) of *Takatsune*, who lived in Kyoto and chiselled guards with pierced decoration. Representatives of the family were working in various parts of the country in the sixteenth century, but their productions had not yet become remarkable. Towards the close of the century *Hideyoshi*, the Taiko, built at Fushimi, overlooking the beautiful valley of the Yodo River, a castle of unprecedented magnificence. The best artistic resources of the time were devoted to the interior decoration of this "Palace of Pleasure," as it was called, and a host of skilled artisans and artists assembled in Fushimi in connection with the enterprise. Few of the works executed for the Palace have survived, but the chiselling of the silver mounts on two state palanquins which stood in the vestibule show that even on such objects the highest skill of the time was expended. It is known incidentally that many experts great in the decoration of sword-mounts worked in Fushimi during the brief period — some ten years — of its prosperity, but the name of one only has been transmitted as directly associated with the place. This artist, *Kanaya*, evidently belonged to the artisan class, for his family name is unknown. He attained re-nown for chiselling landscapes, birds, foliage, and the long, feathery moorland grasses so much affected by Japanese painters and sculptors. His work is compared by Japanese connoisseurs to a moon-lit water-scape seen through an opening in a pine forest.

The seventeenth century was a period of marked development. For the first time during five hundred years the country enjoyed almost complete rest from civil wars, and there sprung up among the various fiefs keen rivalry in the fields of art and industry. One of the fiefs (Kaga) must be specially mentioned in this context. The feudal chief of that province at the time was *Mayeda Toshiiye*. When the Taiko turned his arms against the celebrated warrior *Shibata Katsuiye*, the issue of the combat depended largely upon the attitude of *Mayeda Toshiiye*, then a feudatory of only the second rank. *Mayeda* espoused the Taiko's cause, and as recompense for his fidelity received in fief the whole province of Kaga, thus becoming at once one of the wealthiest and most puissant feudatories in the Empire, while, at the same time, the remote and comparatively inaccessible position of his fief rendered him virtually independent of the government in Kyoto or Yedo. Not unnaturally, therefore, when the tide of political fortune began to set against the Taiko's son, and when Fushimi ceased to be a centre of prosperity, a number of the artists who had settled there turned their faces to Kaga. They were received most hospitably and liberally by *Mayeda Toshiiye*. Kanazawa, the chief town of Kaga, became thenceforth one of the principal centres of art production in Japan, and has retained that distinction down to the present day. The most renowned of the families established there by artists emigrating from Fushimi or Kyoto were the Kuwamura, the Goto, the Mizuno, the Koichi, the Nagayoshi, the Kuninaga, the Yoshishige, the Katsugi, the Tsuji, the Muneyoshi, and the Tadahira. To every one of these houses the Kaga chief granted liberal pensions, varying in amount from the equivalent of 3,500 yen to 250 yen annually. All the early representatives of the Kuwamura family were pupils of the Goto masters and worked in the Goto style, namely, relief chiselling in various metals with addition of gold inlaying. *Moriyoshi*, a pupil of *Goto Kenzo*, was the first recorded member of the house, but it attained the summit of its reputation in the time (1630) of *Hiroyoshi*, who, under his art name of *Koko*, stands in the foremost rank of sword-mount chisellers.

The same description applies to the Mizuno family. Its founder, *Yoshinori*, learned his art under *Goto Yenjo*, and neither he nor his successors made any departure from the methods of the Kyoto masters. It may, indeed, be said that the glyptic movement in Kaga was entirely permeated by Goto influence, and that the greatest artists of this school in the seventeenth century were *Hiroyoshi* (*Koko*), who has just been mentioned; *Kuninaga* (the first, not the second, of the name); *Yoshishige* (1620), a younger brother of *Kuninaga's*, who, as well as *Kuninaga*, had studied under Goto *Takuzo*; and *Uji-iye* (1630) of the Katsugi family, who had the official title of *Gon-dayu*. On the whole, however, the characteristic feature of the Kaga work may be said to have been profuse inlaying with gold. Many Japanese connoisseurs are accustomed to credit *Kuninaga* with having been the first to use gold in-laying in the decoration of sword-furniture. That is an historical inaccuracy. But it is certain that *Kuninaga's* inlaying was so fine as to become proverbial, the term *Jirosaku-hori*— *Jirosaku* was *Kuninaga's* personal name — being used to indicate specially delicate specimens of that nature, to whatever expert they owed their manufacture. Perhaps it will be correct to say that groove-inlaying [*hon-zogan*], as distinguished from surface damascening [*nunome- zogan*], began to be practised with marked success at the beginning of the seventeenth century, for it appears that while *Kuninaga* was winning admiration for such work in Kaga, *Goto Kiyoshi*, his contemporary, was becoming equally famous in the same line in Yedo. The *Nagayoshi* family of Kaga, who began to work when *Kuninaga* was at the zenith of his fame, made groove-inlaying a specialty, and devoted themselves through thirteen successive generations almost entirely to that branch of the art, so that they are generally spoken of as the Kaga Zogan-ko (In-layers of Kaga). It must be noted, further, that *Kuninaga*, *Goto Kiyoshi*, and the *Nagayoshi* experts of Kaga were not the only famous inlayers of the epoch. *Shoami Masanobu* (1620), an artist of Kyoto, produced iron guards with gold-inlaid pictures of the Eight Views of Omi (Lake Biwa), which were the marvel of his time; and *Hosono Masamori*, of Kyoto, working still earlier, —the end of the sixteenth and the beginning of the seventeenth century,— showed such skill in hair-line inlaying (kebori-zogan) that by some authorities he is regarded as the originator of that kind of work.

Masamori would have been remembered for his chiselling in relief, even though he had not distinguished himself specially as a zogan worker. A contemporary of his, *Shoami Nagatsugu*, who lived at Hino in Goshiu, was the first to inlay brass with gold, silver, and shakudo, so that inlaying of that kind came to be known as Yoshiro-fu (Yoshiro style), *Yoshiro* being *Nagatsugu's* personal name. The use of brass as a field for gold or silver damascening does not, when cursorily considered, suggest fine results. But the soft and tender effects of the combination are admirable. Altogether it may be said that the development of inlaying was a feature of art progress at the beginning of the seventeenth century. The history of this century contains so many incidents of importance that it is difficult to marshal them in clear sequence. Certainly one of the most important was the founding of the Yokoya family in Yedo by *Soyo*, who worked from 1621 to 1643. *Soyo* is supposed to have invented the style of chiselling called *kata-kiri*, — that is to say, cutting the lines of a design in channels of varying depth and width, so as to suggest brush-work rather than chiselling. It is impossible to say whether *Soyo* really invented this style or whether he merely brought it into public notice by his great skill. At all events, its extensive practice dates from his time, and it was unquestionably one of the most potential additions made to the art in any era. Speaking broadly, incised chiselling, which had hitherto been mere etching, became thenceforth painting. The Japanese stand quite solitary in this work. They alone among the glyptic artists of the world have carried the element of directness so thoroughly into the ornamental chiselling of metallic surfaces that every line is completed by a single stroke of the tool, and that each line has its own special value in the scale of modelling. *Soyo* received a handsome pension in perpetuity from the Yedo Court. He did not confine himself to kata-kiri work, but carved in relief also with grand force.

His fame is eclipsed, however, by that of his grandson *Somin* (1680-1733), whom many connoisseurs count the greatest chiseller of metal that Japan ever produced. He scarcely deserves such unqualified praise, but he was certainly a grand artist, and in some directions he has never been surpassed. Beginning life with the position of chiseller to the Yedo Court and an annual allowance — hereditary since the time of his grandfather Soyo —

equivalent to about 2,011 yen yearly, he voluntarily resigned the distinction and its associated emoluments, and devoted himself to machi-bori (literally, street carving), or working to general order. This step seems to have been inspired by pure pride of art: he desired to establish an entirely independent reputation for himself, and to owe nothing to the reputation of his family. Like *Goto Yujo*, who had obtained designs from the great painter *Kano Motonobu*, *Somin* sought assistance from two artists famous in his time and in all time, *Tanyu* and *Hanabusa Itcho*. His reproductions of the drawings of these masters by the kata-kiri and kebori processes were so admirable and striking that the public unanimously gave him the credit of having originated the "engraved pictorial style" (yefu kebori), though the conception of such work undoubtedly came from his grandfather *Soyo* and was adopted by his father *Sochi*. It is difficult to speak too highly of *Somin*'s chiselling. There is life in everything that he produced. A spray of peony carved by him contrasts with similar work by other artists as a real blossom contrasts with a paper flower. Accurate examination of his floral work shows that the style of the petal and leaf carving is essentially his own, but that his stalks and branches combine the methods of the Goto and Soyo schools. *Somin* often worked in silver, especially in chiselling kozuka. It may be mentioned here that from the days of the early Goto masters it became a common custom to give a backing of pure gold to kozuka of high quality. *Somin*'s work has always been so much valued by Japanese connoisseurs that few genuine specimens seem to have passed into foreign hands. A noble example was lately sold by the principal art auctioneers in London, but so little did they appreciate it that they grouped it with several ordinary kozuka and sold the whole en bloc! It is possible that many English collectors may thus be entertaining angels unawares.

The celebrated *Nara* family, which deserves and has received at least as much honour as the *Yokoya*, had its origin in the century under review. "*Nara*" is in this case a family name, not the name of a place. *Toshiteru*, an expert of Kyoto and a pupil of the Goto school, was the first metal-chiseller of the family. He moved to Yedo in 1620, but it was not until the time of his son *Toshimune* (art name, *Sotei*) that the Nara workers began to be famous.

Their style was then severe and simple, their favourite designs being crows perched on a withered branch, mandarin ducks in water, birds beside a stream, and such things. *Toshiharu* (art name, *Soyu*, date 1680) abandoned this narrow range of subjects, and became a landscape carver of such consummate skill that the Yedo Court conferred on him the title of Techizen no Kami, and he was thenceforth known in the world of art as *Techizen*. The Nara family gave to Japan three of her greatest artists, *Toshihara* (1680), *Toshihisa* (1720) and *Yasuchika* (1730). The last two do not belong to the seventeenth century, but are mentioned here for the sake of convenience. These three are commonly spoken of as the Nara Sambuku-tsui, or "three pictures en suite of the Nara family." No artists stand higher in Japanese estimation. *Toshiharu*'s art name was *Soyu*; *Yasuchika*'s was *To-u*, and *Toshihisa* is often called *Tahei*, but these appellations are not found upon their works. *Yasuchika* belongs really to the *Tsuchiya* family, but was adopted into the *Nara*. He ranks as the greatest of the three. They all carved in relief, but *Toshihisa* and *Yasuchika* combined the Yokoya style with their own, and carved figures, plants, flowers, birds, and landscapes with extraordinary delicacy and force. *Yasuchika* is sometimes called the "Korin" of carvers, his qualities of boldness, directness, and originality being not less marked than those of the great painter *Ogata Korin*. His works as well as those of *Toshihisa* have been largely imitated, but, as a Japanese connoisseur of the eighteenth century justly says, the imitations differ from the originals as widely as glass differs from diamond. The difference may be illustrated by saying that prior to the Meiji era a good sword-guard by one of the "Three Pictures" sold for the equivalent of from two hundred to four hundred *yen*, whereas an imitation, however skilful, was appraised at about as many *sen*. It should be noted that a great deal of confusion exists between *Toshihisa*, and his teacher *Toshinga*. That is partly due to the fact that the second ideograph of the former's name may be read naga, but also to the fact that *Toshinaga*, though he has received less recognition than *Toshihisa*, can scarcely be called an inferior artist, and that, owing to the number of his pupils, he exercised a lasting influence on the fame of the family. *Toshinaga*'s art name was *Chikan*.

No less than forty-four experts of the Nara school worked between the beginning of the seventeenth and the middle of the nineteenth century, though only six of them were actual representatives of the family. The century was remarkable for a great development of the art of chiselling à jour. That kind of decoration, as already shown, represented almost the only style of the early forgers of sword-guards, and was practised by them with much success. But they treated the guard as though it were a block of cardboard, and were content with the simple operation of piercing, so that the decorative design appeared in outline only. At the end of the sixteenth century, or the beginning of the seventeenth, a new departure was made by adding surface modelling to pierced work. The difference thus produced can be easily explained by saying that whereas a design of cherry petals, for example, took the form of a mere diaper according to the old method, it became, according to the new, a cluster of accurately shaped blossoms and leaves suspended within the circumference of the guard. Under this artistic impulse the guard soon ceased to have the character of a frame, or field, for the design, and was wholly absorbed into the latter. An immense variety of beautiful and cleverly conceived specimens then came into existence. The rim of the guard, ceasing to be rigidly circular, square, or oval, adapted itself to the demands of the design; and the carver, while taking care not to sacrifice the protective purpose of his work, allowed himself wide latitude and irregularity of shape. Thus the "ascending" and "descending" dragons, together with the clouds among which they fly, were disposed so that the backs of the monsters formed the rim of the guard; and a procession of rats pursuing each other in a circle filled all the space surrounding a central haft-socket; or a branch of cherry-bloom, or of plum-blossoms, or of pine-branches, or a cluster of all three combined, was skilfully bent into a circular medallion. Wreaths of iris, sheaves of rice, circlets of intertwined serpents, loops of crayfish, garlands of bean-sprays —

— it would scarcely be possible to enumerate the multitude of notions adopted by the carvers of this school. One of the principal centres of manufacture was the province of Choshiu, the Yamaguchi Prefecture of the present day. As early as the close of the fourteenth century, an expert called *Mitsune* (art name, *Jokan Inshi*) began to work at Suwo in that province, and founded the *Nakai* family. This artist and his immediate successors made no special contributions to the art; they followed the old style of decoration applied to a flat surface. But at the beginning of the seventeenth century *Nobutsune*, a scion of the family, moved from Suwo to Hagi in the same fief, and the work of the Nakai experts thenceforth began to attract wide attention. *Nobutsune*'s grandson, *Tomoyuki* (1660, the first of that name, i.e. *Zensuke*, as distinguished from the second, *Zembei*), and above all his great-grandson, *Tomotsune* (1680), stand in the front rank of chisellers. They carved iron guards with the most elaborately chiselled designs à jour, involving both faces of the guard, their motives being warriors, mythological figures, birds, animals, flowers, landscapes, fish, insects, in short, every natural object that could be utilised for such a purpose. While *Tomoyuki* was approaching the zenith of his fame, an expert of the Umetada family, named *Meiju*, moved from Kyoto to Hagi, and his grandson *Nobumasa* (1690) established the Okada family, which contributed several good artists to the Choshiu school. Another and more important family whose representatives also worked at Hagi, was the *Okamoto*, of which there were two branches, one founded at the end of the sixteenth century by *Tomoharu*; the other, a hundred years later, by *Tomotsugu*. Yet another family was the *Fujii*, founded contemporaneously with the later branch of the *Okamoto* by *Kyokaze*. No detailed reference need be here made to the experts that bore the names of these families. Their work was nearly all in the same style, chiselling à jour with surface modelling; but in comparatively modern times some of them abandoned that fashion and became highly skilled in relief carving of the Kyoto school. The material used by the Choshiu artists was invariably iron, which they tempered and treated with marked ability, the Satsuma workers alone being counted their peers in that respect. Inlaying and picking out with gold were freely resorted to in the decoration of elaborate specimens.

But it is to the *Kinai* family of Yechizen that the seventeenth century owes its finest examples of chiselling à jour. Remarkable as were the achievements of this family, its record is somewhat obscure. The best authorities agree, however, that the first *Kinai* expert worked about the year 1680, and that he was succeeded by five generations of the family. They all used the mark *Kinai*, prefixing the ideograph Yechizen or *Yechizen no Kuni,* and their productions are thus far indistinguishable. But the second *Kinai* (1660) was incomparably the greatest expert of the family. It will scarcely be too much to say that he stands at the head of all Japanese sukashi chisellers. He carved designs à jour in iron with as much delicacy and elaboration as though the material were paper. Of course a sword-guard, which must have a certain degree of solidity and thickness, does not offer the best field for such work. It is in censers — especially clove-boilers — and incense boxes that the most wonderful examples of *Kinai*'s skill are found. These utensils he could cast of wafer-like thinness, decorating them afterwards with pierced patterns fine as lace. Many exquisite specimens were made by him to order of the feudal chief of Yechizen, who presented them to the Court in Yedo. Thus *Kinai*'s chefs-d'oeuvre came to be called *Kenjo Kinai* (presentation Kinai), a term generally applied in later times to all art productions of superlative excellence. The Kinai experts are specially spoken of for supplementing pierced decoration with surface modelling. After the fame of the family had been established, all the sukashi-bori work produced in Yechizen, whether from the *Kinai* ateliers or not, was generally classed as Kinai-bori, though *Kanemori* (1680) and *Chiusaku* 1700), working independently, turned out many examples so good as to deserve distinct mention. The Akao family of Yechizen must also be referred to. Its founder, *Yoshitsugu*, was a contemporary of the first *Kinai*, and worked in the same style. But it is on account of his son, also called *Yoshitsugu*, that the family chiefly deserves to be remembered; for this artist (1670) was the first to employ chiselling à jour in the decoration of shakudo guards. Such work had hitherto been confined to iron, but from *Yoshitsugu*'s time it came to be applied to all metals, shakudo, shibuichi, silver, gold, and brass. This new departure may almost be said to mark an epoch, for by skilful employment of the sukashi process the artist was able to produce effects of atmosphere and space which immensely enhanced the beauty of a design. *Yoshitsugu* subsequently settled in Yedo, and was succeeded by experts of the Akao family through several generations, but none of them attained special skill. At the time of the second *Kinai*, the province of Echizen possessed another artist, *Kogitsune*, who enjoys a great reputation in Japan. Local tradition says that, being ordered to carve a lifelike dragon for the chief of the province, he sat for ten days and nights in the open air at Mikuni, watching the whirlwinds for which that place was remarkable. At last he imagined that he saw a dragon in one of the revolving storms, and the impression was so vivid that he was able to reproduce the monster in iron exactly as he had seen it, a very unusual kind of dragon. Before dismissing the subject of chiselling à jour in the seventeenth century, reference must be made to *Umetada Muneyuki* (1650), a Kyoto expert, who did magnificent work of that nature, several of his master-pieces being made to order of the Shoguns Court in Yedo; and also to the *Ito* family, founded by *Masanobu* in 1670. *Masanobu*, commonly called *Tsuboya Tasuke*, or "Tasuke the guard-maker," lived in Kyoto, and won a high reputation. His son, *Masatsune*, however, was the artist of the family par excellence. He settled in Yedo, received the appointment of guard-maker to the Shoguns Court, and was scarcely inferior to the second *Kinai* as a chiseller of decoration à jour. Representatives of the *Ito* family continued to work in Yedo down to the Meiji era, and one of them, to whom further reference will be made, now ranks among the masters of the era. The *Ito* chisellers followed the lead of *Akao Yoshitsugu*, and worked in shakudo, shibuichi, etc. as well as in iron. In this context reference must be made to a school of experts who worked at Hikone in Omi province. Their style was moulded on that of *Kitagawa Sōden* (Ed. Sōten) (circ. 1640), who forged large iron guards having curved edges, and decorated them with chiselling à jour as well as surface modelling. The peculiarity of these guards was that the figures generally sculptured were those of Dutchmen, Chinese, or some of the uncouth-looking foreigners depicted in ancient Japanese encyclopedias of ethnography. The chiselling was more or less crude and clumsy, and gold damascening was usually added. *Sōden* used the mark *Soheishi*, which is vulgarly pronounced *Mogarashi*. His guards, and those subsequently produced at Hikone in the same style, are commonly spoken of as *Mogarashi-tsuba*.

Among the families which contributed materially to make the seventeenth century remarkable for masterpieces of chiselling in all grades of relief and in the round, with occasional additions, in later times, of the kata-kiri method of the Yokoya masters, a high place must be assigned to the *Yoshioka* of Yedo, founded by *Shigehiro* at the close of the sixteenth century, and brought into prominence by his son *Shigetsugu*, who was appointed to work for the Yedo Court in the year 1600 and died in 1653. The Yoshioka was a noble family of Fujiwara descent, and its early representatives had the titles of Bungo-no-suke and Buzen-no-suke. They did not use these titles in marking their works, but they did frequently use the title Inaba-no-suke. Attached to the employment of the latter there was a restriction characteristic of Japanese customs. The Inaba branch of the same family had a hereditary though conditional right to the high post of court councillor (goroju), and whenever an Inaba noble held that office, the Yoshioka artists were precluded from putting Inaba-no-suke on their works. The restriction happened to be inoperative in the days of *Shigehiro* (called also *Morotsugu*, and, in art circles, *Sotoku*) and *Shigetsugu* (art name, *Soju*), the latter of whom is commonly spoken of, with reference to his carvings, as Inaba-no-suke. His forte was extreme delicacy and fineness. Among the heirlooms of his family is a peach-stone carved by him after an elaborate drawing of a Japanese festival. The preparation of the stone reduced it to about two-thirds of its natural size, and on the scanty surface that remained *Shigetsugu* carved eight boats each carrying an elaborate festival-car, and each manned by thirty-three monkeys. Beside the water on which the boats floated there stood a grove of pine-trees, and under their shadows mandarin ducks sailed, as emblems of love and constancy. Another well-known example of his skill may be seen at the temple *Zojo-ji*, in the Shiba Park (Tokyo). It is a carving on stone, representing the Nirvana of Buddha (*Nehan-ko*), and it was executed immediately after the death of the second Tokugawa Shogun (posthumous name, *Tai-toku-in-deri*), when *Shigetsugu* was in his seventy-third year. The Yoshioka family continued to work in Yedo through successive generations down to the present day, a branch was founded in Sendai in the middle of the seventeenth century by *Kiyotsugu*. No novel features are presented by the Yoshioka carvings they combine the styles of all the schools.

features are presented by the Yoshioka carvings they combine the styles of all the schools. The Isono family, which came into note in the days of *Jochiku* (1630), commonly called *Masuya Bunyemon*, ranked with the Yoshioka masters for minute and delicate chiselling, but were distinguished by more profuse use of gold inlaying. *Jochiku* is considered one of the greatest chisellers of insects that Japan ever produced. His daughter, *Jotetsu*, whose works are spoken of as *musume-bori* (the girl's carvings), was very successful in the same line, as were also several of his pupils and descendants. It was in the early part of this century (1620) that *Hikoshiro*, founder of the Hirata family, began to apply verifiable enamels in the decoration of sword-furniture. Technical knowledge of the enamelling processes existed in Japan before his time, nor does any inventive credit belong to him except in the matter of opaque white enamel, which he was the first to manufacture and which remained a specialty of his family down to recent times. All the other enamels employed by him — green, yellow, blue, red, and purple — were translucid [*suki-jippo*]. Parts of the design were cloisonned, so as to receive the enamels, and much brilliancy of decorative effect was thus produced. The Hirata experts cannot be ranked with Japan's best glyptic artists. The only member of the family who deserves to be called a great chiseller was *Harunari* (1810). For the information of collectors it may be mentioned that sword-mounts having enamel decoration and bearing the Hirata mark are not necessarily identifiable as products of the Hirata family. In the eighteenth and nineteenth centuries, the term Hirata was used to designate a style rather than a family, and artisans often carved it on guards in the former sense. In addition to the families of experts already spoken of as having made their debut in this century, the following may be noted without any detailed reference: — the Tsuji of Yedo, founded by *Masachika* (1660), which produced several generations of skilled experts; the Nomura, also of Yedo, founded by *Masaoki* (1650); the Wakabayashi of Toyama in Yetchiu, founded by *Kaneko Denzaburo* (1690); the Inouye of Kyoto, founded by *Saburozayemon* (1650); the Yasui of Kyoto, founded by *Mitsusada* (1650) and made specially famous by the incomparable chiseller *Nagatsune* (1770), commonly called *Ichi-no-miya Yechizen*; the Chiyo of Tsuyama (in Mimasaka), founded by *Kinsuke* (1680), whose experts produced magnificent silver work;

the Kaneko of Kii, founded by Kichinojo (1640); the Uyemura of Kyoto, founded by Yasunobu (1600) and made celebrated by Masuya Kuhei (1600), and Masuya Kichibei (1720); and greatest perhaps, of all these, the Iwamoto of Yedo, founded by *Chiubei* (1680), a pupil of Yokoya Somin. The century closed when Yanagawa Naomasa, one of the most renowned masters in the whole history of the art, was perpetuating in Yedo the noble style of his teacher Somin.

EIGHTEENTH CENTURY

An immense quantity of beautiful work distinguished this century, and the names of many great experts appear in its annals, but it added nothing to the methods already practised. Scores of skilled chisellers devoted themselves to perfecting the processes of their predecessors without inventing any new technical mode, and, on the whole, it may be said that the distinguishing features of the century were elaboration of detail and splendour of decorative effect. Such developments were consistent with the spirit of the time, for the country had now enjoyed a hundred years of unprecedented peace, and the various principalities throughout the empire, ceasing to be disturbed by problems of military expansion and perils or projects of aggression, had become competitive centres of art production. At the opening of the century *Gorobei* of Kyoto is found chiselling iron guards with decoration à jour so skilfully that the term kinai, which had previously been used to designate particularly delicate and elaborate work of this description was now replaced by *Daigoro-saku*, a name obtained by compounding the first ideographs of *Daimonji-ya*, as the artists' atelier was called, and "*Gorobei*." Contemporaneous with *Gorobei* was *Shoyemon*, called also *Tomoyoshi* or *Yuki*, who has had few peers as a maker of mokume grounds. *Shoyemon* is generally known as *Nomura Masaya*. He entered the service of the feudal chief of Awa, and founded a branch of the Nomura family in Tokushima, the capital of that fief. It should be noted that Yedo was the seat of the elder branch of the Nomura family, which was founded by *Masatoki* (1660), and gave to Japan a number of well-remembered experts, — *Masanori* (art name, *Itoku*, 1790), *Masayoshi* (art name, *Suihaku*, 1760); *Masatsugu* (1760); *Masayoshi* (art name, *Katoji*, 1790), and others.

All these experts excelled in the production of mokume, but were also appreciated for their chiselling in relief. The most celebrated of all the Nomura masters was *Jimpo* (1750), commonly called *Tsu - Jimpo*. He took his designs from the pictures of *Tanyu*, the greatest artist of the preceding century, and his chiselling shows extraordinary minuteness and delicacy. Numerous imitations of his work were produced in the second half of the eighteenth century. Scarcely less renowned was another member of the same family, artistically known as *Hiyobu-jo* or *Yusen* (1790). His literary talents were as great as his glyptic skill, and he received from the Yedo Court the honorary title of Hogen.

It is observable that in this century the artists showed a disposition to make a specialty of particular fields of design. Thus *Shoami Tempo* (1700), of Kyoto, confined himself almost exclusively to chiselling peonies and chrysanthemums tossed by the wind. *Kikugawa Muneyoshi* (1720), of Yedo, commonly called *Chobei*, carved chrysanthemums so admirably that *Chobei-kiku* (Chobei chrysanthemums) came to be a synonym for exceptionally fine work of this class. *Nara Ichibei* (1730), pupil of the great *Nara Yasuchika*, became so celebrated for chiselling the landscapes of Omi that his contemporaries spoke of him as *Miidera Ichibei*. *Nara Masanaga* (1740) obtained equal fame for his moor-scapes with a praying mantis and tufts of soft feathery susuki [Eularia japonica] in the foreground. *Uyemura Munemine* (1720) of Kyoto excelled in the chiselling of warriors. *Yasuyama Motozumi* (1760), of Mito, one of the greatest masters of any era, who was known in art circles as *Sekijoken* or *Togu* chiselled mythological Chinese figures with extraordinary force and delicacy, his favourite metal being shibuichi. *Shinshichi*, of Osaka (1730), chose a fishing-rod and river trout as his specialty. *Noda Yoshihiro* (1730), of Yedo, chiselled groups of fishes with admirable fidelity. *Tamagawa Yoshihisa* (1790), of Mito, made himself famous by his dragons. *Fujita Katsusada* (1700), of Osaka, is remembered for his wonderful masks and cuttle-fish. *Kikuoka Mitsuyuki* (1780), of Yedo, artistically known as *Dopposai* or *Saikaon*, an artist of the highest ability, is held to have equalled Somin as a carver of peonies; and *Shoami Morikuni* (1730), of Matsuyama (Iyo province), has had few equals as a chiseller of dragons and clouds.

This list might be greatly prolonged, but such distinctions are apt to be misleading, since in many cases they suggest a narrower range of motives than the artists in question really selected.

The Nara family made large contributions to the finest productions of this century. *Toshihisa* and *Yasuchika*, who worked during the first half of the century, have already been spoken of, and with them must be bracketed *Joi* (art name, *Issando Nagabaru*, 1720), who by many connoisseurs is regarded as the peer of the "Three Nara Pictures." It is not certain whether *Joi* belonged originally to the Nara family or was adopted into it. He learned carving from *Nara Hisanaga* (art name, *Zenzo*), who, in turn, was a brilliant pupil of the celebrated *Nara Toshinaga*. *Joi* excelled in the shishi-ai style of carving. His work was singularly soft without sacrificing strength, and he chose elaborate subjects, using gold freely for purposes of damascening and picking out. He drew his motives chiefly from martial history, but he chiselled flowers, also, and landscapes with consummate skill. Three other members of the Nara family deserve a place in this context. They are *Masanaga* (1740), his son *Masachika* (1760), and *Masanobu*. *Masanaga* (art name, *Seiraku*) was a pupil of *Toshihisa*. Reference has already been made to his celebrated landscapes with a praying mantis and tufts of Eularia japonica in the foreground. His son, *Masachika*, became a pupil of *Joi* in the latter's old age, and took the art name of *Jowa*. He did not reach the high level of either his teacher or his father, but he was undoubtedly a grand expert. *Nara Masanobu* (1750) had the art names of *Kikuju-sai* and *Kiko*. His works are greatly prized by Japanese connoisseurs, but as his specialty was the carving of the *amariyo* (the rain-dragon), he does not appeal strongly to foreign taste.

At the close of the seventeenth century and the beginning of the eighteenth, Nagasaki's experts were brought into prominence by *Kizayemon*, artistically known as *Jakushi*. Nagasaki, from time immemorial, had been permeated by Chinese influences, being the centre of trade and intercourse between Japan and the neighbouring empire. Hence its chisellers of sword-mounts affected designs generally called kwanto-gata, or Canton style, many examples of which may be seen throughout the whole field of Japanese decorative art.

The familiar "willow-pattern" is the worst specimen of this type. Its features are stiff figures of Chinese warriors, court ladies, mandarins or historical personages, set in a stereotyped garden with architectural accompaniment; or little children — the well known kara-ko (Chinese children) — with tonsured heads, playing various outdoor games; or dragons of more or less conventionalised shape.

Jakushi carved dragons, but he also chiselled landscapes, bamboos tossed by the wind and other designs of flowers and foliage, and his skill was so conspicuous that in Nagasaki people learned to use the term Jakushi-bori as generally distinctive of beautiful work. The use of kwanto-gata motives are not confined to Nagasaki experts. *Goto Kiyonori*, who worked in Yedo contemporaneously with *Jakushi*, became celebrated for similar carving, and examples of it are not infrequently found among the productions of inferior experts. These kwanto-tsuba, and the mogarashi tsuba already described, are, perhaps, the least interesting of all the kodogu. The artists thus far noticed as belonging to the eighteenth century were all representatives of families established at an earlier date. Families which not only gave lustre to the century but also had their origin in it, are the Hamano, the Omori, the Iwamoto, and the Okamoto. These houses produced experts who may be said to have carried the art to its zenith. The Hamano family of Yedo first came into note in the days of *Masayori* (1730), a pupil of the great *Nara Toshihisa*. *Masayori* is always known as *Shozui*, the alternative pronunciation of the ideographs forming his name. He had many art titles — *Otsuriuken, Miboku Rifudo*, etc. He worked chiefly in shakudo, but often in iron, not making any departure from the Nara style, but using his chisels with extraordinary strength yet at no sacrifice of grace and delicacy. The *Soken Kisho* says that the lines of his carving are like "the storm of a tiger's roar or the wind of a dragon's rush through the clouds." It may be truly said of the Hamano family that it did not give one inferior artist to Japan. *Shozui* himself was probably the greatest, but his pupils *Moriyuki* and *Noriyori*, and his successors *Masanobu* (1780) and *Norinobu* (1790) rank almost as his peers. The Hamano artists achieved their greatest successes in figure subjects, but among specimens by *Shozui* there are found some exquisitely delicate and lifelike carvings of bees, spiders, fireflies and herons.

The Omori family of Yedo is generally supposed to have been founded by *Shigemitsu*, who worked in the opening years of the eighteenth century, but his father, *Shirohei*, a samurai of Odawara, was really the first Omori carver. Chronologically, therefore, the family should have been referred to in the notice of the seventeenth century; but it is placed in the eighteenth because it did not begin to be famous until the days of *Shigemitsu*. The latter had the advantage of studying under two of the great Nara masters, *Ichibei* — mentioned above as "*Miidera Ichibei*" — and *Yasuchika*. He carved with great skill in the Nara fashion. It was by his pupil *Terumasa*, however, that the style of the Omori family was fixed — namely, a combination of the Nara and Yokoya methods, with extreme elaboration of detail and profuse use of all decorative adjuncts, such as inlaying and picking out with gold, silver, copper, etc. *Terumasa* received instruction from the great *Somin* (*Yokoya*) as well as from *Shigemitsu*, and would doubtless be remembered as a most distinguished artist had not his fame been completely eclipsed by that of his adopted son, *Teruhide* (1748—1798), known in art circles as *Ittosai* or *Riu-u-sai*. *Teruhide* was a grand chiseller. Some of his high-relief peony sprays in gold on shakudo are not inferior to Somin's masterpieces. He is said to have been the first to carve wave diaper in high relief, and to him was due a splendidly decorative ground of shakudo inlaid with gold in the aventurine pattern. The *Soken Kisho*, says of *Teruhide*: "His chiselling has force that would rend a rock. His wave diapers deeply carved in shibuichi are magnificent, and nothing could exceed the beauty of his peonies in high relief on aventurine grounds. He seems to have based his method of carving flowers on *Somins* celebrated ichirin-botan (single-blossom peony). His martial figures also are grand." It may be said that peonies and Dogs of Fo [*shishi*] were *Teruhide*'s specialties. Among ten choice examples of his work in a Tokyo collection, only two are without peony flowers either in the principal or a subordinate place. Many artists bore the family name after *Teruhide*'s time, but although their work was of the finest quality from a decorative point of view, they scarcely merit special mention on account of their glyptic skill.

Concerning the Iwamoto family of Yedo the same remark applies as that made about the Omori, namely, that although founded in the seventeenth century, it did not become famous until the eighteenth. The founder was *Chiubei* (1680), a pupil of the celebrated *Yokoya Somin*, and the family's greatest master was *Konkwan* (1760-1801), who is counted one of Japan's most skilled chisellers of fishes of all kinds (especially Crustacea), but who also carved with admirable ability wild-fowl, insects, flowers and even figures. *Konkwan* had three art names, but he seems to have always marked his pieces *Iwamoto Konkwan*. The productions of the Iwamoto experts were not so elaborately decorative as those of the Omori, but as an artist *Konkwan* is certainly not inferior to *Teruhide*. It is recorded that during the latter years of his life the Iwamoto master was so besieged by clients that he finally hung out this sign: "Orders cannot be quickly executed. Importunity is deprecated." The Okamoto family of Kyoto was a branch of the great *Okamoto* of Hagi (Choshiu), already alluded to. It was founded in 1750 by *Harukuni* (originally called *Kuniharu*), who is known in art circles as *Tetsuya-ya Dembei* (Dembei the Iron chiseller). *Harukuni* worked in iron. Although the representatives of his family in Choshiu were celebrated chiefly for chiselling à jour, he reduced that kind of decoration to a subordinate position, and relied more upon relief carving in all its grades, as well as upon the kata-kiri method. Indeed, by *Dembei*'s time the experts of Kyoto and Yedo had ceased to make à jour chiselling the principal feature in a decorative scheme. They preferred to utilise such work with reference to its pictorial suggestiveness. Thus a delightful effect of space and atmosphere is produced by clouds chiselled à jour, with a silver moon struggling through them, its disc revealed in the open spaces and concealed by the solid rack; or the sheen of water is obtained by a delicate outline of transparent carving; or the leaves and branches of a tree are projected against the sky by cutting out all intervening portions. Even when the à jour feature predominated, it was always associated with decoration carved in the round, so that it served chiefly to detach the sculptured object from the flat surface. One of the most illustrious artists of this century, or indeed of any century, was *Kashiwaya Nagatsune* (1750-1786), called in art circles *Setsuzan* or *Ganshoshi*.

It is difficult to conceive a higher standard of force, accuracy, and grace than he attained. He seems to have worked almost entirely on shakudo and shibuichi bases, but he used gold, silver, and copper freely for decorative purposes. In his early days the objects that he preferred to chisel were frogs, snails, beetles, and so forth, and generally he added a tuft of the grass called tsukushi (a species of horse-tail). But he subsequently extended his range to dragons, figures, demons, masks, and other objects, and among his numerous works, all of which are highly valued in Japan, there is not one of inferior quality. His Deva Kings, chiselled in high relief in shakudo with gold decoration, may be compared to the celebrated wooden statues at the temple Kofuku-ji. Japanese connoisseurs liken the nobility and purity of *Nagatsune*'s style to "the moon rising over Obate mountain." In recognition of his exceptional talent he was honoured by the Kyoto court with the title of Daijo of Ichi-no-miya in Yechizen. His son, *Nagayoshi*, did not fall greatly short of *Nagatsune* himself in ability. Both worked in Kyoto. The only remaining names that need be especially referred to in the history of the eighteenth century are those of *Kusakari Kiyosada* (1790), generally known as *Kusakari Hachisaburo*, who is said to have been the greatest inlayer that ever worked in Sendai; *Shichibei* (1700) of Kyoto, whose fame as an inlayer procured for particularly fine work of that nature the term *Zoshichi*; and *Ito Kiyoyasu* (1750) of Yedo, the first to become celebrated for the variety of inlaying called sumi-zogan.

NINETEENTII CENTURY

By more than one Western critic of Japanese metal-work it has been asserted that a period of decadence set in before the middle of the nineteenth century, and that all productions subsequent to the year 1835 or 1840 show evidences of deterioration. It would be very difficult to discover any valid grounds for such a statement, nor is it endorsed for a moment by Japanese connoisseurs. Everywhere dilettanti may be found whose estimate of the merits of a work of art ascends with the cycles that have elapsed since its production. But that kind of picturesque romance belongs to a special domain of Aesthetic education, and while its contentions are partially admissible so long as they refer to a *Somin*, a *Yasuchika*, a *Naomasa*, or a *Kinai*, they must be set aside ruthlessly when they do flagrant injustice to the numerously peopled school of fine artists in metal who worked for Japan during the first seven and a half not the first three decades of the nineteenth century. And in speaking of the first seven and a half decades, it is not intended to suggest that the year 1875 saw the end of her artistic metal-work. On the contrary, the reader already knows that the art has merely developed new phases in modern times, and that not only are its masters as skilled now as they were in the days of the Goto, the Nara, the Yokoya, and the Yanagawa celebrities, but also that their productions must be called in many respects greater and more interesting than those of their renowned predecessors. If sword-mounts alone be considered, the year 1876 may be taken as the time of the art's demise, for in 1876 the wearing of swords was interdicted and purchasers of their furniture were at once reduced from hundreds of thousands of samurai and privileged persons, to a few scores of foreign curio collectors. Thousands of grand specimens found their way at once to the melting pot for the sake of the modicum of precious metal that could be extracted from them, and in an incredibly short time the multitude of master-pieces that must have existed in 1876 disappeared almost completely. The fate of that great assemblage of beautiful objects is indeed a mystery. Hundreds of skilled experts had been engaged continuously during five centuries on their production; millions of samurai had taken a pride in their possession, and the objects themselves were imperishable. Yet in less than thirty-five years they virtually ceased to be procurable in Japan. It is true that a considerable number went to Europe and America, and that an equal, or perhaps even a larger, number remained in Japanese collections. But what comparison can be set up between the petty fraction thus accounted for and the vast multitude that must have existed at the moment when the edict of 1876 went forth? This is one of the most curious pages of the iconoclastic chapter opened simultaneously with the opening of Japan to foreign intercourse. As the old order changed, the beauties it had bequeathed to the country were swept away with the blemishes it had begotten; and if the process was sometimes slow in the latter case, it was often almost miraculously rapid in the former. Incredible though the fact may seem, it is nevertheless a fact that when, about the year 1880, United States' collectors began to interest themselves keenly in Japanese sword-mounts, and to acquire them in the resolute manner of New York and Chicago, the supply of genuine specimens could not meet this fitful and comparatively paltry demand, and the forger drove a brisk trade for a season, casting where he could not chisel, and substituting flash and profusion of ornament for force and delicacy of sculpture. To day, an amateur applying himself in Japan to make a representative collection of fine sword-mounts could not hope for more than very partial success. Those that are already fortunate in the possession of such objects may therefore congratulate themselves, for while in every other branch of Japanese art no serious break has occurred in the continuity of successful production, the sword-mount is altogether a thing of the past and will never again occupy the attention of great sculptors. As to the assertion made above that sword-mount experts continued to work with undiminished skill down to the year 1876, a better illustration cannot be adduced than that of *Goto Ichijo*. The reader will probably have observed that, in these records of centuries, no reference is made to the Goto family. It is not to be inferred, of course, that the omission indicates absence of merit or of celebrity. But at the outset considerable space was devoted to the Goto masters, and it has not seemed necessary to speak subsequently of the various experts born in the branches of the family; for although many of them were great carvers, they did not originate any new style, and the indications given in the appended list of Glyptic Artists are probably sufficient to show the Gotos' share in the development of the art. It may be explained here, however, that in addition to the principal family and its two great branches in Kyoto the Kami-Goto and the Shimo-Goto there were in that city two minor branches; in Kaga a branch founded by *Ichiyemon*, a pupil of *Kenjo*, in 1610; and in Noto a branch founded in 1550 by *Jinyemon*, a pupil of *Takujo*. *Goto Yeijiro*, afterwards known as *Goto Ichijo*, was born in 1791 and died in 1876. The second son of the fifteenth representative of the principal family, he was adopted into the branch house of *Hachirobei* (art name, *Kenjo*), to whose hereditary pension of fifty koku of rice he succeeded in 1805, taking the names *Mitsuyo* and *Hachirobei*. When only nineteen years of age he received a commission to carve mounts for a sword belonging to the Emperor *Kokaku*, and he succeeded so well that the title of Hokkyo was accorded to him, together with a reward of twenty pieces of silver and five bundles of silk. In his thirty-fourth year he was invited to Yedo by the Tokugawa Court, received a house and a perpetual pension of ten rations, which was afterwards increased from time to time, until, in 1862, he attained the highest art rank, that of Hogen. *Ichijo* had no less than fifty pupils, all of whom worked with considerable success. Among them was occasionally numbered *Natsuo*, who probably deserves to rank next to *Ichijo* among the masters of the nineteenth century. *Ichijo* has left it on record that in his youth he made a habit of praying at the shrine of Fushimi Inari that the deity would grant him skill. One night after his devotions, he fell asleep and saw in a dream a dragon carved by his illustrious ancestor, *Goto Yujo*. Thenceforth he had before his eyes a perfect model of a dragon. His workmanship, however, was finer than anything done by *Yujo*. Japanese connoisseurs say that it combines the soft style of *Goto Kwojo* with the microscopic minuteness of *Goto Kenjo*, and a story is told that a party of skilled experts being challenged to name the maker of a set of sword-mounts by *Ichijo* without seeing the name carved on the back, were divided in opinion as to whether the work should be ascribed to *Kwojo* or to *Kenjo*. These details furnish some indication of the career of a great Japanese carver, and of the honours extended to him. There was, indeed, no limit to the appreciation he received. Among the archives of *Ichijo*'s family there is a letter addressed to the artist by *Okubo Toshimitsu*, one of the leading statesmen of the Restoration. It is couched in terms of the most profound politeness; it speaks of *Ichijo*'s work as beautiful enough to "move the gods to tears"; it declares that the specimens just completed at the writer's request shall be treasured by him and his heirs so long as the house of Okubo lasts. The incentives that talent found in those days can thus be appreciated. *Ichijo* certainly deserved to be famous. He excelled in every kind of chiselling, though most of his finest work is in relief; he knew how to produce admirable decorative effects by combining metals of various colours; his range of motives was almost limitless, and the poetic feeling of some of his designs gives them a charm quite independent of their grand technique.

The difficulty experienced in attempting to set down any record of the metal-workers in the nineteenth century is that quite an embarrassing number of artists reached a standard entitling them to notice. The greatest do not stand as far above the general level as did the masters of preceding epochs, but, on the other hand, the general level in the nineteenth century was higher than it had ever been before. It can be said with confidence, however, that no school of experts contributed so much to the treasures of the time as did the representatives and disciples of the Ishiguro family. According to strict chronological order, this family should have been included in the annals of the eighteenth century, for its founder, *Masatsune*, who also must be called one of its greatest representatives, was born in 1757 and died in 1828. He is placed here, however, not only because much of the finest work of his mature years was executed in the nineteenth century, but also because all his successors and pupils flourished during the latter. The Ishiguro family carried the art to an extreme standard of elaboration. No subject was too intricate or too difficult for them, and it is probable that their works figure largely in foreign collections, for technical beauty and richness of general effect are qualities which appeal at once to the average dilettante. *Masatsune* had three art names *Jimiyo*, *Togakushi*, and *Jikokusai* and during his youth he called himself *Koretsune*. He is thus often confounded with his second son, *Koretsune*, an equally great artist, the confusion being augmented by the fact that among *Koretsune's* seven art names *Togakuski*, *Ritsumeiy Shinryo*, *Hogyokusai*, *Gisbinken*, *Kounken*, and *Ichiyeian* the first was identical with one of *Masatsune's*. No less than forty-two experts belonged to the Ishiguro group, and every one of them contributed some good specimens to the treasures of the century. After *Masatsune* and *Koretsune*, the most renowned were *Koreshige* (art name, *Ichio*), a pupil of *Koretsune*; *Koreo* (art name, *Hakuunshi*), also a pupil of *Koretsune*; *Yoshitsune* (art names, *Senyushi*, *Gammon*, and *Tominsai*), grandson of *Masatsune*; *Masayoshi* (art name, *Jikosai*), a student of *Masatsune*; Koreyoshi (art names, *Jikakushi* and *Kwansai*), son of Masayoshi; Yoshisato (art name, *Jitekisai*), a pupil of *Masayoshi* who worked in Hizen; *Haruaki*, who received the highest art title of Hogen; *Masahiro* (art names, *Gantoshi*, *Keiho*, *Kwakujusai*, and *Korinsha*), a pupil of *Masatsune*;

Masakiyo (art name, *Jikiyokusai*); *Masaharu* and *Kiyonari* (art name, *Giyokkosai*). All of these, with the one exception noted in its place, worked in Yedo. With the Ishiguro experts must be bracketed, in point of technical skill, the three families of Omori, Hamano, and Iwamoto. The origin of these has already been spoken of, and it will be sufficient to note here the celebrities that they severally contributed to the nineteenth century, namely:

THE OMORI MASTERS AND THEIR PUPILS IN THE NINETEENTH CENTURY

Hidetomo; art name, *Riuriusai*. Yedo.

Hideyoshi; art name, *Ittokusai*. Yedo.

Hideyori. Hirado (Hizen).

Hidenori. Hirado.

Hidetomi. Sendai.

Hidekiyo. Yedo.

Kazutomo; art name, *Kenkosai*. Yedo.

Tomochika; art name, *Riunsai*. Yedo.

Tomotsune. Yedo.

Terumoto. Yedo.

THE HAMANO MASTERS AND THEIR PUPILS IN THE NINETEENTH CENTURY

Shunzui, or *Haruyori*. Yedo.

Juzui, or *Hisayori*. Yedo.

Shuzui, or *Hideyori*. Yedo.

Kiuzui, or *Hisayori*. Yedo.

THE IWAMOTO MASTERS AND THEIR PUPILS IN THE NINETEENTH CENTURY

Konju. Yedo.

Kwanri (end eighteenth /beginning of nineteenth century). Yedo.

Yeishu, or *Yasuchika Shinsuke* (end eighteenth /beginning of nineteenth century). Celebrated for Katakiri chiselling. Mito.

Riyoyei, or *Suzuki Kinyemon*. Celebrated for carving fish. Yedo.

Kwanjo.

Shoho, or *Buto Gempachi*, marked his works *Konkwan-mon*. Yedo.

The productions of the four families, Omori, Hamano, Iwamoto and Ishiguro, stand to the master pieces of the early metal-carvers in much the same relation as the genre pictures [*ukiyo-ye*], which had their development contemporaneously with the work of these families, stand to the paintings of the classical school. In reviewing Japanese pictorial art it has been shown that the popular school of painters, the Ukiyo-ye artists, were a natural outcome of the social evolution of their era, and that they reflected the nation's passage from the comparatively austere canons of a military age to the voluptuous ease and refinement of the later Tokugawa epochs. Similar evidence of the changes of the times might be expected to present themselves in the field of glyptic art. They do present themselves. The formal designs and uniform methods of chiselling à jour practised up to the middle of the fifteenth century represent the pure Chinese style, or, at any rate, were suggested by the classical spirit which then permeated every branch of the national civilisation. By and by, when the immortal painters *Kano Masanobu* and *Kano Motonobu* raised their art into a new realm of national inspiration, a corresponding impulse was felt in the domain of metal carving, and the Goto masters, shaking themselves partially free from classical fetters, began to seek decorative motives in the pages of recent history or among the natural objects that surrounded them. The work of the early Goto experts cannot, however, be assigned purely to any one academy. In their representations of historical scenes, warriors, and animals they followed the Tosa school with almost slavish accuracy. In their carvings of flowers, birds, and incidents from the daily life of the people, they took the Kano artists for models. And in their chiselling of dragons, Dogs of Fo, Kylin, phoenixes, and supernatural beings, they saw nothing higher than Chinese types. They preserved, indeed, a closer touch with the Chinese school than with any other, for each scion of the family and each student in its ateliers commenced his education by learning how to carve a dragon, and in every Japanese collection of Goto masterpieces the shisbi, the kirin, and the ho-o repeat themselves persistently. But even *Yujo* himself did not recognise any limit to his range of motives, and, as has been already seen, he and his descendants must undoubtedly be credited with having opened a new vista to their art.

The Nara school was the next link in the chain of evolution. Faithful to the fashions of the era in which it had its birth, it made a still wider departure from the classical style than the Goto experts had attempted, and drew its inspiration from the Kano and the Tosa schools only, combining the strength, realism, and softness of the former with the decorative splendour of the latter. The Yokoya masters went a step farther. It is true that they may be said to have revived the Chinese spirit, since linear force, directness, and vitality became, in their hands, paramount elements of glyptic skill. But in that respect they stand to their own branch of art as the Kano painters stood to theirs; if they followed the technical methods of the Chinese school, they derived their motives chiefly from Japanese life and annals. Side by side with the Yokoya masters, and in many respects closely connected with them, the Yanagawa, Kikuoka, Kikuchi, Yoshioka, and Kikugawa families produced works which correspond with the pictures of the naturalistic school of Kyoto, the Shijo academy, which had its greatest representative in *Maruyama Okio*. Then finally came the four families forming the popular school, the Omori, the Hamano, the Iwamoto, and the Ishiguro, to whom *Goto Ichijo* must be added as an unsurpassed master of their style. It is difficult to convey in words any general idea of the luxury of decoration, delicacy of chiselling, poetry of motive, and, withal, simplicity of subject exhibited in the masterpieces of experts like *Omori Teruhide, Iwamoto Konkwan, Hamano Noriyuki, Ishiguro Masatsune*, and many of their disciples and followers, as well as their contemporary artists of the naturalistic school. Perhaps the best plan is to describe briefly a few specimens which may be regarded as fairly illustrative. Here, for example, is a kozuka by *Ishiguro Koreyoshi*. The metal is shibuichi and the ends are tipped with gold. It may be noted, that many of the finest kozuka produced in the eighteenth and nineteenth centuries have their ends and backs of gold, though the face is shakudo, shibuichi, or even copper. The kozuka in question is made throughout of shibuichi, except the gold-shod ends, but the back is richly inlaid with gold in the style called kiribaku (cut leaf); tiny squares of gold are scattered evenly over the whole field. On the face is chiselled, in high relief, a hawk which has just lighted among the branches of a blossoming plum, and in the distance a sparrow is seen flying away (Ed. not illustrated).

The hawk's grey plumage is excellently suggested by the patina of the shibuichi, and its feathers and crest are etched with a delicate damascening of gold. The plum blossoms are softly chiselled in silver, and the sparrow's russet colour is well rendered by the copper in which it is modelled. The reverse has this couplet engraved in cursive script :

"Gone the old year,
Gone to his death;
Tears for his tomb.
Yet from his bier
Stealeth spring's breath
Of wafted plum."

(The plum-blossom is the emblem of spring.)

[kozuka by Ishiguro Koreyoshi, Hawk hunting a Goose]

Here, again, are two kozuka by *Goto Ichijo* (Ed. not illustrated). The first is of copper backed with gold. On the face, beautifully modelled in medium relief, are two golden mummers of the New Year, dancing, instinct with life, and above their heads the conventional decorations of the season hang, incised. On the back these lines are engraved:

"Endless the ages shed on earth
Their gems of joy. Once more in truth
The jewel of a year's new birth,
Flashes the light of laughing youth
From fount and well. Each quickened tree
Gives pledge of leafy luxury.
A myriad signs of gladsome springs
And years untouched by pain or ruth (grief)
For you, my prince, this sunrise brings."

The second kozuka is of shakudo, wrought on both faces with fine-grained nanako. The design, chiselled in low relief and painted, no other term applies to the skill of the manipulation, painted with gold, silver, and bronze, is the rustic gate of a country cottage, overhung by pine-trees, and standing among feathery grasses of autumn. The tender restfulness of the picture is delightful. On the back are these lines:

> *"One are our hearts, my wife's and mine.*
> *Beyond the reach of withering years,*
> *Beyond the sound of falling tears,*
> *To skies spring sunshine always fills*
> *The music of our love notes thrills,*
> *Through the linked branches of the pine."*

(The pine-tree is one of the emblems of longevity.)

Reference may finally be made to a kozuka and a kogai chiselled by Watanabe Hisamitsu, a prominent representative of the popular school. Here the designs correspond exactly with pictures by *Kiyonaga* or *Utamaro*. On the copper face of the kozuka, chiselled in relief, is the celebrated "lady of the green hall," *Takao*. She is magnificently apparelled, and gold, shakudo, silver, and shibuichi are used with the most refined skill to indicate the rich brocades and crepes that she wears. On the Kogai the same courtesan is shown in gentle dalliance with the ascetic *Daruma*. The backs of the kozuka and Kogai alike are of shibuichi, carrying the following inscriptions:

"Buddha sells doctrine. The expounder sells Buddha. The priest sells the expounder. You sell your five feet of body to nurture the lusts of humanity. Green is the willow; crimson the flower; many-coloured the ways of the world."

> *"A thousand nights, a thousand eves,*
> *The soft moon sails the lake above;*
> *No trace of her caresses leaves,*
> *In the cold depths no ray of love."*

In this century the Hirata family spoken of already as the first to employ verifiable enamels in the decoration of sword-mounts had its greatest master in the person of *Harunari*. One of his pupils, *Uchino Harutoshi* (art name, *Ichigenshi*), was scarcely less celebrated, and four others helped, in a lesser degree, to perpetuate his fame. Later in the century Yedo produced an artist of the very highest skill, *Kano Natsuo*. He worked from 1850 to 1895, and certainly deserves to be called one of the most admirable chisellers of incised designs that Japan has known in any era. *Natsuo* learned the art, from *Aoka Harutsura*, of Kyoto, himself a skilled expert; and *Harutsura's* teacher, *Kajutsura*, deserves to be mentioned as an exceptionally successful chiseller of insects. *Natsuo's* early works were chiefly chiselled in medium relief. His range of subjects was wide. He could represent a group of autumn flowers, a spray of plum, or a tiny insect as skilfully as a mythological figure or a historical scene. After fame and prosperity had come to him, he ceased to carve in relief, and confined himself to incised and kata-kiri chiselling, with results of which it would be difficult to write in too laudatory a strain. He did not easily accept an order or make any effort to produce largely. Genuine specimens of his work are therefore rare, and when one comes into the market, it is purchased by Japanese connoisseurs at a great price. Contemporary with *Natsuo* in the latter's early years was *Honjo Yoshitane*, of Yedo. He not only chiselled the mounts of swords but also forged their blades, and he is placed by his countrymen in the very foremost rank of artists. *Yamagawa Koji*, of Kanazawa (in Kaga), was another of the most prominent figures in the nineteenth century. He worked from 1830 to 1877, chiefly in the kebori and kata-kiri styles, and in his later years he received the name of "*Kanazawa Somin*" in recognition of his great abilities. The Mito school was very active in the first half of the century. Several well-known experts were connected with it as *Kwaizantei* (*Motomichi*) and his numerous pupils; *Ontaiken* (*Motochska*); *Chooken* (*Motonari*); *Tosuiken* (*Sadahisa*), and others.

The workshops in Aizu also turned out many specimens, but what has already been said of Mito and Aizu work in earlier times applies to the productions of the nineteenth century also: it was decorative rather than artistic. Many other names might be set down; notably those of *Yoshioka Tadatsugu*, of Yedo, whose pupils constituted a large and brilliant group; *Tanaka Kiyohisa*, of Yedo; *Okano Kijiro*, of Yedo, widely known under his art name of *Toriusai*, whose reproductions of some of the choicest old masterpieces are probably treasured by many Occidental collectors as originals; *Kawarabayashi Hidekuni* (1860), of Kyoto; and *Oda Noaki* (1830), of Satsuma, a splendid chiseller of decoration à jour. But the task of discrimination becomes exceedingly difficult in the nineteenth century, for although the general level of expert skill was higher than it had been in any previous era, few artists can be said to have attained conspicuous pre-eminence. An immense number of fine specimens were produced during the first seventy-five years of the century, and it is probable that if a careful examination were made of the best collections of Japanese sword-mounts in Europe and America, a great majority of the examples they comprise would be found to date from the epoch 1770 to 1780. Special mention must be made of a group of five artists *Shuraku*, *Temmin*, *Riumin*, *Minjo*, and *Minkoku* who, in 1864, formed a guild (called Go-nin-gumi) for the purpose of producing objects beyond the strength of other experts. Their style was chiefly kata-kiri and in addition to sword-furniture they turned out a quantity of kana-mono, that is to say, minor metal work of all descriptions. These men were all of the highest force.

(Ed. Although described, no illustrations of tsuba or fittings were in the original book, other than those displayed on opposite page, following is a lengthy list of 'Chisellers' unfortunately no Japanese kanji was included.)

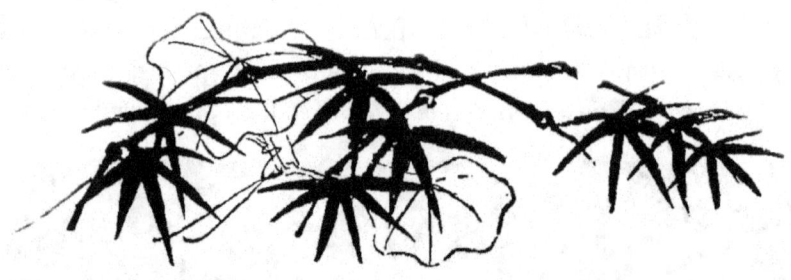

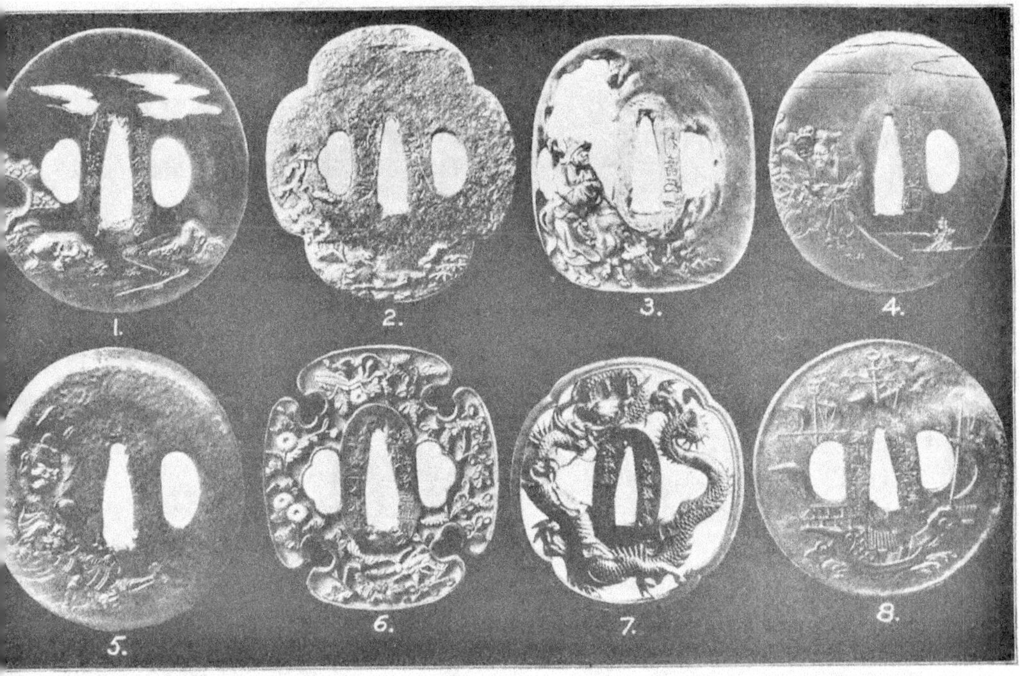

SWORD GUARDS I.

By Tsuchiya Yasuchika.   4. By Hamano Kōzui.   7. By Hagidani Katahei.
By Jakusai.   5. By Sugiura Tai.   8. By Nakai Tomotsune.
By Nara Toshihis.   6. By Kitagawa Sōten.

SWORD GUARDS. PLATE II.

1. & 4. By Nara Toshihisa.   3. By Yanagawa Naomasa.   6. By Miyochin Muneakira.
2. By Umetada Shigeyoshi.   5. By Nara Toshiharu.   7. By Yokaya Sōmin.

79

ALPHABETICAL LIST OF CHISELLERS OF SWORD-FURNITURE

Adachi. Yusai. 19th cent. Yedo.

Akao. Family name: vide Yoshistugu Tashichi.

Akihiro. 19th cent. Yedo.

Akushi. Tamagawa. 1700. Founder of the Tamagawa family of Mito.

Aoki. Family name: vide Harustura.

Aoyagi. Family name: vide Yoshimitsu.

Arakawa. Ikki. 19th cent. (d.1895). A Tokyo metal-chiseller of the highest skill.

Arichika. Kimura. 1850. A skilled artist of Tokyo, pupil of Yasuchika (the 6th generation from To-u).

Arinobu. 19th cent. Owari.

Aritsune. 19th cent. Yedo. Art name, Kakutei.

Asanji. Watanabe. 1780. Toyama.

Atsuoki. 18th and 19th cent. Art name, Sensai.

Atsuoki. Sasayama. 1860. Art name, Ichigyosai. A Kyoto expert of high rank. One of the best carvers of the 19th cent.

Ayabe. Masayuki. 19th cent. Yedo.

Bikwan. Vide Katahiro.

Bunji. 1700. An expert; in the service of the feudal chief of Owari.

Bunjo. Goto. 1690. Kyoto.

Bunsui. Yoshida. 1650. At first called Nomura Rokubei. A pupil of Goto Renjo, an expert of the first rank. Specimens bearing his name are found not infrequently, but they are all forgeries, as he is known never to have marked any of his work. Kyoto.

Buzen. Yoshioka. 1740. An artist who worked for the Tokugawa Court. Yedo.

Chiba. Tomotane. 19th cent. A metal-worker of Yedo.

Chikaatsu. Yoshioka. 1690. Otojiri. Yedo.

Chikatomo. Yoshioka. 1670. Wakichi. A pupil of Kiyasugu. (Yoshioka.) Yedo.

Chikatsugu. Yoshioka. 1700. Yedo.

Chikayoshi. Ishiguro. 1840. Mannosuke. Yedo.

Chikuzanken. Vide Matosada. (Ogawa.)

Chiruiken. Vide Takahiro. (Yasui.)

Chitomo. Chiyo. 1760. Called also Chiusuke. An expert of Tsuyama.

Chiubei. Iwamoto. 1680. Founded the Iwamoto family of Yedo. Worked in Yedo.

Chiubei. Tokaya. 1700. A pupil of Somin. Yedo.

Chiubei. 1650. Saburohei. A skilled artist of Kaga, in the employ of the feudal chief of that province.

Chiusaku. 1700. An artist of Yechizen, who worked skilfully in the Kinai style.

Chōbei. Kikugawa. 1720. Muneyoshi. An artist of the highest skill in the Shizumebori style. He chiselled flowers, especially chrysanthemums, with such ability that the term Chobei-Kiku came to be generally applied to fine work of that class (Chobei chrysanthemum). His son and grandson had the same name and worked in similar style. Yedo.

Chōjō. Goto. 1590. Commonly called Shichibei. Son of Goto Kojo and founder of the Kami-Goto family, Kyoto, and afterwards Mino.

Chokuzui. Vide Naoyori.

Chōkwaku. Goto. 1700. Nothing certain is known about this expert. He is said to have been adopted into the Shoami family, and he worked in Kyoto.

Chōōken. Vide Motomori (Nemoto).

Chōroku. Shoami. 1820. An expert of Aizu.

Chōsendo. Vide Terumitsu (Omori).

Chounsai. Yoshitane. 19th cent. A metal-worker of Yedo.

Daimonji-ya. Vide Gorobei.

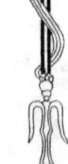

Daisuke. Shoami. 1530. Founder of the Oshiu branch of the Shoami family. Morioka (Nambu).

Dempachi. Muneta. 1650. Kyoto.

Denjō. Goto. 1570. Called also Mitsuhiro, son of Goto Tokujo. Kyoto.

Dennai. Shoami. 1600. An expert of Akita (in Dewa).

Denzaburo. Wakabayashi. 1690. Called also Kaneko. Toyama.

Denzaburo. Kaneko. 1690. A pupil of Goto Tsujo. Worked at Toyama (Yetchiu).

Denzaburo. Yokoya. 1780. Called also Tamotake, Yedo.

Dōnin. Vide Hikoshiro. (Hirata.)

Dopposai. Vide Mitsuyuki. (Kikuoka.)

Dōriu. Hasebe. 1640. A pupil of Goto Yechijo. Residence uncertain.

Fuchō. Dainichi. 1750. An expert of Osaka, whose work is much admired by Japanese connoisseurs for chasteness and delicacy. He had some reputation as a poet.

Fujii. Masahiko. Present day. Metal sculptor. Pupil of Unno Shomin.

Fujiki. Vide Masayuki (Tsuji).

Fujiwara. Kiyotoshi. 19th cent. Metal-worker of Yedo.

Fukawa. Kazuo. Present day. An eminent metal-sculptor.

Fukushige. Shoami. 1580. Worked in Owari, after the style of Yamayoshibei.

Fūkō. Vide Takanaga (Yasui).

Fumiyo. 1890. Art name, Kansai. A pupil of Natsuo; considered one of the best recent chisellers of iron guards.

Funada (Katsutani). Nakazawa. 19th cent. Skilled metal-worker of Yedo. Art name, Ikkin.

Funakoshi. Shummin. Present day. A great metal-chiseller who adopts the styles of Matsuo and Shomin. A pupil of Ikedo Minkoku, who had been taught by Haruaki (q.v.).

He took the two ideographs Haru (Shun) and Min to form his art name of Shummin. His chiselling is very fine, and he is admirably skilled in repoussé work.

Fusamitsu. Vide Yeiju.

Fusanao. Fujiki. 1690. Called also Kobachi. A pupil of Goto Shujo (Mitsutaka), Yedo.

Fusanori. Miyochiu. 1560. A skilled expert. Kamakura.

Fusayori. Hamano. 1790. Kiuzo. Known also as Yeizui. A skilled expert of Yedo. Art name, Riyochiken.

Fusayoshi. Miyochin. 1550. A great expert. Especially celebrated for chiselling chrysanthemums à jour. Worked in Kozuke and also in Kiushiu.

Gakan. Fuse. 1610. A pupil of Goto Yeijo. Kyoto.

Gammon. Vide Yoshitsune.

Ganshoji. Vide Nagatsune.

Gantoshi. Masuhiro.

Geki. 1750. A skilled expert of Sendai, where chiselling is very delicate.

Gekkindo. Vide Masatatsu.

Gembei. Uyemura. 1720. A pupil of Munemine. His house was known as Masuya. Kyoto.

Gempachi. Goto. 1620. Kyoto.

Gempachi. Mizuno. 1650. A skilled expert, but died very young. Kaga.

Genchin. Furukawa. 1680. Kichijiro. Also called Shoju. A pupil of Somin. He carved admirably in his master's style. (Katakiri.) Yedo.

Genji. Mizuno. Vide Teruyoshi.

Genjō. Goto. 1550. Younger brother of Kojo, the 4th Goto master. A great expert, generally spoken of as Goto Kumbei. Kyoto.

Genjō. Goto. 1550. Kyoto.

Genjō. Goto. 1690. Called also Mitsuyoshi and Kambei. Kyoto.

Genjō. Goto. 1630. Sometimes called Kakujo. Kyoto.

Genjō. Vide Narimasa.

Genju. 19th cent. Metal-worker of Yedo. Art name, Taizanken.

Genjūken. Vide Motoharu (Katoji).

Gen-no-jo. Goto. 1670. Kyoto.

Genroku. Mizuno. Vide Mitsumasa.

Genshichi. Mizuno. 1650. A skilled expert, but died very young. He and Gempachi were sons of Yoshinori-Kaga.

Gentaro. Goto. 1690. Kyoto.

Genyemon. Goto. 1690. Called also Mitsuhisa. Kyoto.

Gishinken. Vide Koretsune.

Giyemon. Kimura. 1670. A pupil of Goto Kambei. Kyoto.

Giyokuriuken. Vide Katsushiro.

Gokokuzan. Mitsunaka. 18th and 19th cent. A skilled worker of Yedo.

Gon-no-jō. 1780. A pupil of Iwamoto Kwanri, and a skilled expert. Sendai.

Gorobei. 1700. His house was called Daimonjiya. A celebrated guard-maker, whose decoration à jour was of the most elaborate and delicate character. His works came to be called "Daigoro-tsuba," a term subsequently synonymous with particularly choice open-work chiselling. Kyoto.

Goro-saku-bori. Vide Yoshishige.

Goroyemon. Ukai. 1740. A skilled expert of Osaka; the teacher of Fucho.

Goto. Yoshinori. 18th and 19th cent. Yedo.

Goto. Mitsuyoshi. Vide Yenjo.

Goto. Denjo. 19th cent. Yedo.

Goto. Mitsubumi. 19th cent. Yedo.

Goto. Tojo. 19th cent. A skilled worker of Yedo. Received the art title of Hokyo.

Goto. Yoshitoru. Present day. A skilled metal-chiseller of Osaka.

Gyokkeisha. Vide Masayori.

Hachibei. Tokita. 1630. A pupil of Goto Yekijo and a fine expert. Kyoto.

Hachirobei. Goto. 1790. An expert of one of the Kyoto branch families of the Goto. Art name, Kenjo.

Hakuhōtei. Vide Kankwan.

Hakuunshi. Vide Koreo.

Hakushusai. Vide Masanaka.

Hamano. Chiku-yuki. 19th cent. A metal-worker of Yedo.

Hambei. Inouye. 1750. A pupil of Inouye Shigeyasu. Kyoto.

Hankeishi. Vide Masayori.

Haruaki. Kono. 1830. Chuizo or Bunzo. Art names, Geisuo, Sanso, Taio. A pupil of Yanagawa Naoharu. Had no fixed place of abode, but worked chiefly in Yedo. A contemporary of Goto Ichijo and one of the greatest experts of the 19th century. Attained the title of Hogen.

Haruchika. 18th and 19th cent. Metal-worker of Yedo.

Haruhiro. Nakamura. 1820. Itahei. A pupil of Harunari (Hirata). Yedo.

Hamhisa. Nishimura. 1820. Ginjiro. A pupil of Harunari (Hirata). Yedo.

Harukuni. Okamoto. 1760. Dembei. An artist of great reputation, whose skill in manipulating iron was such that he received the name of Tetsuya Dembei (Dembei the iron-worker). He founded the Okamoto family of Kyoto, and was the teacher of the still more celebrated Tetsuya Gembei. In early life he called himself Kuniharu. Kyoto.

Harumasa. Otsuka. 1820. Shichibei. A pupil of Harunari (Hirata).

Harunari. Hirata. 1810. Hikoshiro. Eighth and best of the Hirata experts. Called also Tomokichi. Yedo.

Harushige. Yanagawa. 1860. A skilled expert of Yedo; teacher of Koji of Kanazawa.

Harutomo. Omura. 1820. A pupil of Harunari (Hirata). Yedo.

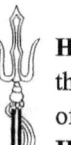

Harutoshi. Uchino. 1820. Tojiro. called also Ichigenshi. A pupil of Harunari and a skilled expert. Yedo.

Harutsugu. 1820. A pupil of Harunari (Hirata). Yedo.

Harutsura. Aoki. 1830. A Kyoto expert of the very highest skill. Teacher of the celebrated Natsuo. His works are among the finest of the 19th century.

Haruyori. Hamano. 1810. Ginjiro. A skilled expert generally called Shunzui. Yedo.

Hashimoto. Isshi. 19th cent. Metal-worker of Yedo; very skilful and prolific.

Heisuke. Shoami. 1770. Heishichi. An expert of Tsuyama in Mimasaku.

Hideaki. Ishiguro. 1850. Kinjiro. Yedo.

Hidechika. Nomura. 1779. A pupil of Masahide (Nomura). His real name was Ichikawa Magohei. Yedo.

Hidekatsu. Shoami. 1770. An expert of Matsuyama in Iyo.

Hidekiyo. Komatsu. 1800. Sennosuke. A pupil of Teruhide (Omori). A celebrated expert. Yedo.

Hidekuni. Kawarabayashi. 1860. A Kyoto expert of great skill. Art name, Tenkodo.

Hidemasa. Shoami. 1740. An expert of Matsuyama in Iyo.

Hidemasa. Nomura. 1780. Denzayemon. Original family was Yano. Awa.

Hidemitsu. Omori. 19th cent. Metal-worker of Yedo.

Hidenori. Vide Sōden (Sōten). According to some authorities, Hidenori and Sōden (Sōten) were distinct, and both worked in the same style at Hikone.

Hidenori. Shiraishi. 1800. Denkichi. A pupil of Teruhide (Omori). Worked at Hirado in Hizen.

Hideo. Naomaru. Vide Onishi.

Hideoki. Omori. 19th cent. Metal-worker of Yedo.

Hidesaburo. 1760. One of the pupils of the Akao family, who carved in the style of Yoshitsugu Kohei. Yedo.

Hideshige. Tsuchiya. 18th cent. Metal-worker of Yedo.

Hidetake. Yoshioka. 1670. Kizayemon. Generally known as Yoshioka Kizayemon. A pupil of Yoshioka Kiyotsugu, and a skilled expert. Sendai.

Hidetomi. Kusakari. 1800. Kiuzo. A pupil of Teruhide (Omori). Sendai.

Hidetomo. Omori. 1800. Sadabei. Called himself Riurinsai. A pupil of Teruhide (Omori), and a skilled expert. Yedo.

Hidetsugu. Uyemura. 1740. Ihei. A pupil of Takafusa (Uyemura). Kyoto.

Hideyasu. 19th cent. Metal-worker of Yedo.

Hideyori. Hayata. 1800.

Heishiro. A pupil of Teruhide (Omori). Worked at Hirado in Hizen.

Hideyori. 1810. Commonly called Shuzui. Yedo.

Hideyoshi. Omori. 1800. Kitaro, and sometimes called Sakai Itsuki. Called himself Ittokusai. A pupil of Teruhide (Omori), and a skilled expert. Yedo.

Hikokoro. Vide Yasuyuki.

Hikoshiro. Hirata. 1620. Called Donin. The first to employ cloisonne enamels in the decoration of sword-furniture. Such work became thence-forth a specialty of the Hirata family. Yedo.

Hikoshiro. Wakabayashi. 1740. Son of Kokusui, and an expert of note. Toyama (Yetchiu province).

Hirakuni. 1650. Sanyemon. Kaga.

Hirakuni. Akao. 1810. An expert of Sendai who carved in the style of Tempo.

Hirata. Soko. Present day. A skilled uchimono-shi of Tokyo.

Hirayori. Hamano. 1810. Commonly called Kiuzui. Yedo.

Hiroaki. Ishiguro. 1850. Zenkichi. Yedo.

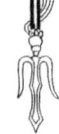

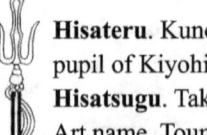

Hiromasa. 19th cent. Metal-worker of Yedo. Art name, Toju.

Hirosada. Miyochin. 1850. Art name, Kingyokudo. A skilled expert of Yedo. Remarkable for making shakudo dragons with rounded scales. Often used the mark Cofu Saishin.

Hirotoshi. Otherwise called Kwanri.

Hirotoshi. Uchikoshi. 1810. Yenzo. Originally known as Konishi Bunshi-chi. Art name, Ichijosai. A great expert of Kyoto. Studied under Yoshinaga (Tamagawa).

Hiroyoshi. Kuwamura. 1630. Sazayemon. A great expert. Pupil of Goto Teijo. He was appointed to work for the Daimyo Daishoji Hida-no-Kami, and had an annual allowance of 100 Koku of rice. He called himself Koko, and afterwards Joku. Kaga.

Hiroyori. Murata. 1750. Ikujiro. Known also as Kwanzui. Called himself Ichiyōken. Yedo.

Hisachika. Ishiguro. 1840. Kanejiro. Yedo.

Hisaharu. Suzuki. 1810. Tetsujiro. A pupil of Kiyohisa (Tanaka). Yedo.

Hisakiyo. Hamano. 19th cent. Metal-worker of Yedo.

Hisakiyo. Goto. 1670. Shichibei. A skilled expert. His carvings of grapes and bees on fuchi and kashira are celebrated. Kaga.

Hisamitsu. Watanabe. 1810. Chiu-goro. Art name, Tokosai. A pupil of Kiyohisa (Tanaka). Yedo.
N.B. The name is also pronounced Toshimitsu.

Hisanaga. Nara. 1710. A pupil of Toshihisa. Some of his carvings are marked Denzo. An expert of great skill. Yedo.

Hisanori. Nara. 1770. Signed many of his works Unteido. Yedo.

Hisateru. Kunesake. 1810. Ginjiro. A pupil of Kiyohisa (Tanaka). Yedo.

Hisatsugu. Takahashi. 1820. Kanejiro. Art name, Tounsai. Aizu.

Hisatsugu. Yoshioka. 1640. Rizayemon. At first called Shigeyoshi. Third son of Shigetsugu. Yedo.

Hisayori. Nara. 1760. Yedo.

Hisayori. Hamano. 1800. Hanai. Commonly called Juzui. Yedo.

Hiyobu. Hogen. Nomura. 1790. Posthumous name, Minamoto Masayori. Artistically known as Yusen or Hi-yobu-jo. and called in literary circles Shjoishi-gekkaan-koo. Eldest son of Masahide (Nomura). He received the honorary title of Hogen in recognition of his artistic skill.

Hiyōji. Kawakami. 1770. Toyama (Yetchiu).

Hōgiyokusai. Vide Koretsune.

Hōjō. Vide Mitsuaki (Goto).

Hōjō. Goto. 1670. Mitsukata. Kyoto.

Hōju. Vide Tomihisa. Hokiusai. Vide Naofusa.

Honjo. Vide Narikado.

Horiaki. 18th cent. Metal-worker of Yedo.

Horiuken. Vide Takani. Yeiji.

Hosuiken. Tsuchiya. 18th and 19th cent. Metal-worker of Kaga.

Hozanken. Vide Motonori (Yasuyama).

Huzui. Vide Yasuyori and Toyoyori.

Ichibei. Nara. 1730. Pupil of the celebrated Yasuchika. He was known as "Miidera Ichibei," on account of the beauty of the landscapes of the temple of Miidera carved on his fuchi and kashira.

Ichiga. Yamazaki. 1770. Niziyemon. There were five experts called Ichiga. The first flourished in 1670, and was a pupil of Goto Shujo; the fifth, at the close of the 18th cent. All were fine carvers. Kyoto.

Ichigenshi. Vide Harutoshi

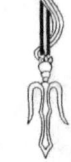

Ichigyosai. Vide Atsuoki.

Ichijiusai. Vide Mitsutatsu.

Ichijō. Goto. One of the greatest experts of the 18th cent. Born, 1791; died, 1876. Taught in Kyoto, but worked in Tokyo. Received the title of Hokyo in recognition of his skill.

Ichijū. Takeshima. 1600. Tozayemon. A pupil of Goto Tsujo. A splendid artist, standing in the highest rank. Yedo.

Ichimudo. Vide Terutoki. (Omori.)

Ichirobei. Yamada. 1700. An expert of Nagasaki who made guards of the Kanto-tsuba style; namely, decorated with Chinese figures and landscapes.

Ichiroyemon. Tanaka. 1700. A skilled artist of Satsuma.

Ichiruisai. Vide Tomoyoshi. (Kiku-gawa.) Ichiso. Kawada. 1720. A Satsuma expert.

Ichiunsai. Vide Masayoshi.

Ichiyeian. Vide Korestune.

Ichiyemon. 1610. A pupil of Goto Yetsujo. A skilled expert. Kaga.

Ichiyodo. Vide Mitsuyori.

Ichiyoken. Vide Hiroyori.

Ichizayemon. Fukui. 1660. A pupil of Goto Yetsujo. A skilled artist. Kaga.

Ichizō. Vide Nariyuki and Narisuke. Ihei.

Inouyc. 1750. A pupil of Inouye Shigeyasu.

Ikedo. 19th cent. (d. 1897.) A great metal-chiseller of Tokyo. One of the last carvers of sword-furniture.

Ikken. Present day. A skilled metal-chiseller of Tokyo.

Ikkin. Funada. 1840. Shosuke. An artist of skill who studied for some time under Goto Ichijo and finally worked in Kyoto.

Inaba-no-suke. Yoshioka, A title borne by four celebrated artists of the old Yoshioka family; namely, Shigehiro (1600), Yasutsugu (1610), Kiyotsugu (1630), and Terutsugu (1680), and by those of lesser note in modern times.

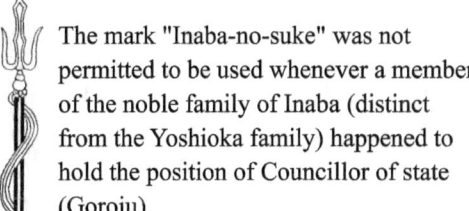

The mark "Inaba-no-suke" was not permitted to be used whenever a member of the noble family of Inaba (distinct from the Yoshioka family) happened to hold the position of Councillor of state (Goroju).

Inagawa. Family name. Vide Naokatsu and Yoshikatsu.

Injō. Goto. 1620. Mitsutomi. Kyoto.

Iranken. Shoami 1570. An expert of Owari.

Ishin. Shoami. 1800. An expert of Matsuyama in Iyo.

Issai. Vide Tokiakira.

Isshiken. Vide Okinari.

Issho. Nakagawa. 1860. A skilled artist of Yedo.

Isshunan. Vide Masyori.

Itao. Shinjiro. Present day. A highly skilled metal-chiseller of Kagawa (in Kishiu). He manufactures iron dragons, eagles, crabs, etc. with universal joints, as skilfully as did the great Miyochin Yoshihisa, and many of his masterpieces have been sold in foreign markets as Miyochin's work. Formerly he was employed solely by Yamanaka, the well-known dealer of Osaka, and subsequently by Sano of Tokyo.

Ito. Vide Masanaga and Masatsune.

Ito. Shoyei. Present day. Metal-sculptor. Pupil of Unno Shomin.

Ito Katsumi. Masatatsu. Present day. A metal sculptor of the highest skill. Tenth representative of the Ito family founded by Ito Masanaga, who with all his descendants, down to the present representative, were makers of sword guards for the Tokugawa Shoguns. A pupil of the celebrated Toriusai, his early years (he was born in 1829), were devoted to chiselling sword-furniture. In 1860, he was adopted into the Ito family, his rival for that honour having been the equally celebrated Kano Natsuo.

From 1864 he was directed by the Shoguns to inscribe the name Katsumi upon his guards, etc., but in later years he used the mark Taikiu. After the Restoration (1867) he devoted his chisel to carving metal objects suited to the changed tastes of the time; as plaques, paper-weights, book-markers, etc.

Itoku. Vide Masanori.

Ittoku. Tsuji. 1750. Gendayu. Art name, Ransuido. An expert of Omi.

Ittosai. Vide Teruhide (Omori). Iwama. Masayoshi. 19th cent. A metal worker of Yedo.

Iyefusa. Miyochin. 1560. Pupil of the celebrated Nobuiye, and a great expert. Odawara.

Iyehisa. Miyochin. 1600. A great expert. Sagami.

Iyemori. Shoami. 1790. A kyoto expert skilled in inlaying with gold.

Iyenori. Saotome. 1550. A pupil of the celebrated Nobuiye and a skilled expert. Hitachi.

Iyesada. 1560. Highly skilled for chiselling à jour. Said to have been a pupil of Nobuiye.

Iyesada. Shoami. 1670. An expert of Matsuyama in Iyo.

Iyetaka. Vide Shigeyoshi Tsunetada.

Izawa. Tadatsura. 18th cent. (d.1875). A metal-worker of Nagoya, particularly skilled in producing the tama-mokume grain; which is obtained by putting balls (tama) of different metal into a cylinder, heating the latter red, and then beating the whole mass together.

Jakui. Vide Katsuhisa. (Kuwamura.)

Jakushi. Vide Kizayemon.

Jichikuken. Vide Motonaga, (Ogawa).

Jidayu. Wakabayashi. 1710. Ozawa. Toyama.

Jikakushi. Vide Koreyoshi.

Jikiyokusai. Vide Masakiyo.

Jikokusai. Vide Masatsune.

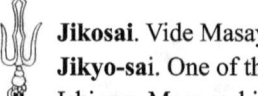

Jikosai. Vide Masayoshi.

Jikyo-sai. One of the art names of Ishiguro Masayoshi.

Jimiyo. Vide Masatsune.

Jimpo. Nomura. 1750. Tsu Hachiyemon. Generally known as Tsu Jimpo. A pupil of Masanori. (Nomura.) A grand artist; one of the greatest masters. He died in 1762 at the age of 52. Kyoto. (Many imitations of his work exist.)

Jingo. 1630. A guard-maker of Yatsushiro. His specialty was inlaying iron with brass designs in high relief. Hence guards in that style are called jingo-tsuba.

Jinyemon. Vide Mitsuaki.

Jinyemon. Goto. 1550. Founded the Noto branch of the Goto family, but afterwards lived and worked in Kaga. A great expert.

Jiriuken. Vide Teruaki. (Yokoya.)

Jiriuken. Miyaki. 1720. A pupil of Soyo. His early work is mediocre, but in his later years he carved grandly. Yedo.

Jiriuken. Vide Tsuneyuki.

Jiriusai. Vide Toshiharu.

Jiriyusai. Vide Tsuneyuki.

Jiro-saku-bori. Vide Kuninaga and Yoshishige.

Jitekisai. Vide Yoshisato.

Jitsujō. Goto. 1660. Kyoto.

Jiujiro. Suzuki. 1840. A skilled expert of Tokyo.

Jiuyemon. Kurose. 1650. A pupil of Goto Renjo. Kyoto.

Jizaburo. Tamagawa. 1800. Worked in Mito.

Jizan. Vide Nagayoshi.

Jōchi. Sasaki. 1630. Shobei. A pupil of Goto Yenjo. Kyoto.

Jōchiku. Isono. 1630. Originally called Matsuya Bunyemon, but afterwards Kozayemon. A celebrated expert both as a carver and as an inlayer. Kyoto.

Jōchin. Furukawa. 1790. A skilled expert, even better than his father Genchin. His carving is generally incised, but sometimes in relief. Yedo.

Jōchiu. 1640. A pupil of Jochiku and almost as fine an expert. The works of the two men are often confounded. He was subsequently adopted by Jochiku. Kyoto.

Jōha. Goto. 1580. Mitsunobu. Kyoto.

Jōhaku. 1640. Wasuke. A pupil of Jochiku and a skilled expert; afterwards changed his name to Shoyei. Yedo.

Joi. Nara. 1720. One of the greatest masters. A pupil of Nara Zenzo (Hisanaga). He displayed extraordinary skill in shishi-ai carving, and is considered the peer of the "Three Nara Masters." Vide Toshihisa. He sometimes marked his works Issando Nagaharu. Yedo.

Jōkan Inshi. Vide Mitsutsune.

Jōken. Goto. 1680. Mitsuyoshi. Kyoto.

Jokū. Vide Hiroyoshi.

Jokwo. Torii. 1740. Uhei. Commonly known as Masuya Ukei-Osayka.

Jomi. Yeizuke. Present day. A great metal-worker of Kyoto, (b.1839). Celebrated for vases of woven metals; for various beautiful patinas; and for plaques with elaborately chiselled landscapes. Jomi is his art name; Yasuchika his personal name.

Jōrin. Goto. 1630. Uhei. A skilled expert of Osaka. Called also Mitsunari. Kyoto.

Jōriu. 1640. A pupil of Jochiku. Yedo.

Jōsen. Goto. 1620. Kyoto.

Jōshin. Goto. 1540. The third of the great Goto masters. Kyoto.

Jōshiu. Vide Mitsutomo.

Jōtetsu. Isono. 1660. A daughter of Jochiku. Her work is generally spoken of as Musume-bori, or "the girls' carving." Kyoto.

Jōtoku. 1650. Date uncertain. A Yedo expert, supposed to have been a pupil of Jōchiku.

Jōunsai. Vide Shiratoshi.

Jōunsai. Vide Kwanri.

Jōwa. Vide Masachika (Nara).

Jōyeiken. Vide Takakiyo (Sakawa).

Jōyeiken. Vide Yoshihisa.

Jōyen. Goto. 1600. Kyoto.

Jōyen. Fujii. 1660. A pupil of Goto Renjo. Kyoto.

Jōyen. Fujinaka. 1700. A pupil of Masanori Nomura. Yedo.

Jōyo. Goto. 1670. Mitsuchika. Kyoto.

Jōzui. Vide Sukeyori.

Jubei. Aoki. 1580. Generally regarded as the second generation of Kaneiye. Was employed by the feudal chief of Higo and settled at Hasuike. Art name, Tetsujin. A great expert, remarkably skilled in the making of iron guards. He inlaid some of his guards with brass.

Jugyokusai. This art name was originally used by Katsuyoshi, and now employed by his pupil Yoshikawa Issei; both metal-chisellers in the Ishiguro style.

Jujō. Goto. 1720. The twelfth Goto master.

Junjō. Goto. 1650. Called also Mitsuakira. Kyoto.

Jūzō. Vide Kiyotoshi.

Jūzui. Vide Hisayori.

Kagawa. Katsushiro. Present day. A highly skilled metal-chiseller of Tokyo; pupil of Mori Ryoken and of Matsuo. He spent five years chiselling a five branched Paullownia within a square of 0.18 in. side for the furniture of a sword belonging to the Emperor.

Kagawa. Katsushiro. Present time. A highly skilled worker in metal. Famous for chiselling naturalistic subjects as plaques, vases, etc., using several metals. Has been employed to carve sword furniture for the Emperor.

Kageiye. Miyochin. 1560. A celebrated expert. Sagami.

Kahei. Mori. 1700. A pupil of Yanagawa Naomasa. Yedo.

Kaigunshi. Vide Kaneyuke.

Kaijo. Goto. 1620. Mitsutsune. Kyoto.

Kaijo. Goto. 1660. Mitsukatsu. Kyoto.

Kaizantei. Vide Motochika. (Hayama.)

Kajima. Ippu. 19th cent. (d.1860). A metal-chiseller of Yedo, who made kanamono, ita-gusari, ojime, etc.

Kajima. Ippu. Present day. One of the greatest metal-workers of the century. From 1855 to 1887, he produced only sleeve links, bracelets, broaches, etc. for the foreign market, making them of iron inlaid with gold in the Nunome style. But from 1887, he began to manufacture the now celebrated Toge-dashi-zogan.

Kajima. Yeijiro. Present day. A metal-worker of Tokyo, skilled in inlaying. A cousin of the much more celebrated Kajima Ippu. Yeijiro's father of the same name produced some fine specimens of inlaid armour.

Kajutsura. 1820. A skilled expert of Kyoto; teacher of Harutsura. Celebrated for chiselling insects.

Kakō. Vide Hirayoshi (Kuwamura).

Kakujō. Goto. 1590. Mitsunobu. With Mitsusato and Mitsumasa, he makes the three Mino-bori (Mino carvers) of the Shimo-Goto Family. Mino.

Kakuriyo. Tsuji. 1780. Heishiro. Called himself Shisuido. An expert of note. Omi.

Kakutei. Vide Aritsune.

Kambei. Goto. 1670. Mitsutoyo. The Kami-Goto Family. Kyoto.

Kambei. Goto. 1690. Vide Genjo.

Kampei. Nishigaki. 1730. A carver of Higo.

Kanamaru. So-no-shin. An unidentified artist.

Kanaya. 1600. An artist of Fushimi. Celebrated for his carving of landscapes, birds, foliage and prairie-grasses. His work is compared by Japanese connoisseurs to a moonlit waterscape seen through an opening in a forest.

Kaneatsu. Takao. 1640. Kichizayemon. A pupil of Umemura Sukesaburo and a skilled expert. Kaga.

Kanehide. 19th cent. Yedo.

Kaneiye. 1500. A celebrated guard-maker whose date is somewhat uncertain. He marked his work Yamashiro-no-ju. His tempering and chiselling of iron were counted extraordinarily good, and in subsequent generations special luck was supposed to attend the possession of his guards, so that they commanded great prices. Japanese connoisseurs consider that the Kaneiye family forged guards before the time of the above, and they are accustomed to speak of the older work as "Osho-dai Kaneiye" (the very old generation of Kaneiye). Vide Jubei (Aoki).

Kaneko. Vide Ujiiye.

Kanemori. 1680. An expert of Yechizen, who worked skilfully in the Kinai style.

Kanemori. Shoami. 1550. An expert of Kaneda in Dewa.

Kanenori. Nomura. 1720. Saburoji. Called himself Kanyeishi. A skilled expert. Hikone. (Omi.)

Kanesada. 1600. Supposed to have been a pupil of Aoki Jubei.

Kanetaki. Yoshikawa. 1680. Called also Tamayoshi. Worked at Hikone.

Kanetomo. Iwata. 1810. Bennosuke. Art name, Toyosai. Pupil of Kiyohisa (Tanaka). Aizu.

Kaneuji. Shoami. 1750. A Kyoto expert.

Kaneyasu. Masatoshi. Metal chiseller (Kinzokushi) of present day. A pupil of Toriusai (q.v.) and adopted son of Ito Katsumi (q.v.)

Kaneyori. Amano. 1760. Son of Shozui, and commonly called Kenzui. Art names, Kaigenshi, Miseki, and Seishin. Used also the marks Otsu-riuken and Miboku. (Vide Shozui.) A celebrated artist. Yedo.

Kaneyuki. Hamano. 1670. Called himself Kaiganshi, and afterwards Miboku. A son of the celebrated Shozui. Yedo.

Kankyo. Vide Masayori and Masanobu.

Kanshikan. Vide Terukazu.

Kanshiro. Nishigaki. 1750. A carver of Higo.

Kanyeishi. Vide Kanenori (Nomura).

Kanzayemon. Nishigaki. 1770. A carver of Higo.

Kariuken. Vide Yoshinori.

Kasetsuken. Vide Tomonao.

Katahiro. Nomura. 1760. Bikwan. Yedo.

Katatomo. Nakano. 1830. A skilled forger of swords and chiseller of sword-guards. Especially remarkable for combining various metals. Yedo.

Katsu. 1700. A female expert of Yedo. Her work is good, but nothing definite is known about her.

Katsuchika. 19th cent. A great metal-worker of Yedo, and chiseller of netsuke.

Katsuhira. 19th cent. Yedo.

Katsuhisa. Kuwamura. 1650. Genzayemon. Called himself Jokui. An expert of great repute. Kaga.

Katsuiye. Miyochin. 1550. A great expert. Kozuke.

Katsukata. Shoami. 1670. Chiuzayemon. Worked at Wakamatsu in Aizu. Katsukuni. 18th and 19th cent. Mito.

Katsukuni. Shinozaki. 1750. Tokuro. A skilled expert; one of the best of the Mito artists. (Vide Yasuhira.) Mito.

Katsumasa. Miyochin. 1540. A great expert. Kozuke.

Katsumi. Ito. 1860. A great artist, still living, but now better known for miscellaneous work than for sword furniture.

Katsumori. 19th cent. Metalworker of Yedo.

Katsunari. Shoami. 1620. Worked at Wakamatsu in Aizu.

Katsusaburo. Shoami. 1700. There were two experts of this name, father and son, the latter being also called Gorobei. They worked at the close of the 17th and the beginning of the 18th century, and were skilled silver-smiths. Tsuyama (in Mimasaka).

Katsushiro. 18th and 19th cent. A skilled metal-worker of Yedo. Art name, Giyoku-riu-ken.

Katsutada. Fujita. 1700. An artist of Osaka, notably skilled in carving masks and cuttle-fish.

Katsutane. Kanasugi. 19th cent. Art name, Shokatei. Yedo.

Katsuyoshi. 19th cent. Art name, Rakurakusai. Yedo.

Kawada. Family name. Vide Ichizo.

Kawaji. Tomomichi. 18th and 19th cent. Choshiu.

Kawasaki. Tashiro. Present day. A skilled metal-chiseller of Tokyo. Pupil of Natsuo. Remarkably clever in working out naturalistic designs, as carp, ai (river trout), etc., for pouch-clasps.

Kazuharu. Ishiguro. 19th cent. Metal-worker of Yedo.

Kazunori. Omori. 19th cent. Yedo.

Kazutani. Kanasugi. 19th cent. Art name, Kenkosai. Yedo.

Kazutomo. Omori. 1810. Yetsusuke. Called himself Kenkosai. A skilled expert. Yedo.

Kazutoshi. Kishiba. 19th cent. Yedo.

Kazutsune. Omori. 19th cent. Metal-worker of Yedo. Son of Kazutomo; and same art name as his father.

Kazuyuki. Kumagaye. 1840. Goro. A pupil of the celebrated Goto Ichijo, and a skilled expert. Yedo.

Keiho. Vide Masahiro.

Keijō. The fourth representative of the Goto family. Vide Mitsumori.

Keirinsai. Vide Yasuhisa.

Keisai. Vide Masatsune.

Keito. Vide Masayori.

Kenjō. Goto. 1610. Seventh of the great Goto Masters. Kyoto.

Kenkōsai. Vide Kazutomo, Kazutani, and Kazutsune.

Kensui. Vide Masanao.

Kenzui. Vide Kaneyori and Hisayori.

Kichibei. Uyemura. 1720. Commonly called Masuya Kichibei. A pupil of Munemine (Soho), Kyoto.

Kichibei. 1730. One of the pupils of the Akao family.

Kichiguro. Tamagawa. 1820. Worked in Mito.

Kichijuro. Tamagawa. 1780. A pupil of Yoshihisa of Mito and a skilled expert, though his works are little known.

Kigu. 1750. Family, etc., unknown, and date uncertain. The name is often found on good specimens having carp, crawfish, etc., in relief on a polished ground.

Kihei. Inouye. 1750. A pupil of Inouye Shigeyasu. Kyoto.

Kihei. Goto. Vide Zenjo.

Kijusai. Vide Terumitsu (Omori).

Kikkōdō. Vide Naoyasu.

Kikō. Vide Masanobu.

Kikuchi. Family name; vide Tsunekatsu, Tsunemitsu, etc.

Kikuda. Mitsugiyoku. Present day. A highly skilled metal-chiseller of Tokyo; employed by the Imperial Court. He carved a celebrated silver handwarmer (Shuro) for the Emperor, decorated with designs of wisteria.

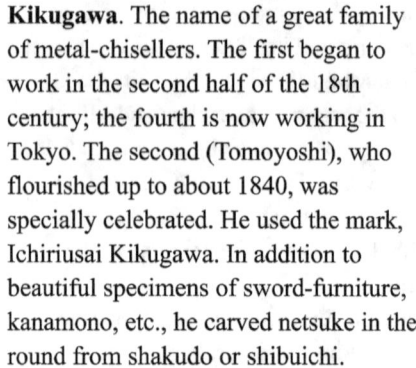

Kikugawa. The name of a great family of metal-chisellers. The first began to work in the second half of the 18th century; the fourth is now working in Tokyo. The second (Tomoyoshi), who flourished up to about 1840, was specially celebrated. He used the mark, Ichiriusai Kikugawa. In addition to beautiful specimens of sword-furniture, kanamono, etc., he carved netsuke in the round from shakudo or shibuichi.

Kikuju-sai. Vide Masanobu (Nara).

Kikuoka. Family name. Vide Mitsuyuki.

Kinai. Ishikawa. 1640. An expert of Ichizen who belonged originally to the Miyochin family. He was celebrated for chiselling iron guards with designs à jour, his favorite designs being dragons and phoenixes. His works are marked Yechizen no Kuni Kinai. He died in 1680.

Kinai. Takahashi. 1660. The second of the same name and the greatest of the family. His pierced decoration on guards is admirably delicate and fine, and he imparted to the iron a soft, brown patina of great beauty. His works were known as Kenjo Kinai, or "Presentation Kinai;" that is to say, worthy to be presented to the Sovereign. He prefixed to his name the words, Yechizen no Kuni. He died in 1696.

Kinai. Much of the work produced in Yechizen after the time of the two great Kinai masters is spoken of as "Kinai," meaning that it is in the Kinai style. Vide Chiusaku, Yoshitsugu, and Kanemori. The successive representatives of the Takahashi family produced good work in the same style.

Kingenshi. Vide Sadayoshi.

Kingyokudō. Vide Hirosada.

Kinkadō. Vide Mitsutaki.

Kinriuzan. Fumoto. Vide Shigemitsu (Omori).

Kinshichi. Tsuchiya. 1650. A pupil of Katsuhisa (Kawamura). Kaga.

Kiriusai. Vide Muneyuki; also Somin.

Kiriusei. Vide Soyoyuki.

Kiso-Hōgen. Vide Koriusai.

Kiujo. Goto. 1630. Mitsutada. Kyoto.

Kiukiuken. Vide Tamagawa Yoshihisa.

Kiusuke. Chiyo. 1680. There were three experts of this name, father, son, and grandson. They worked chiefly in silver. Tsuyama (in Mimasaka) .

Kiuzayemon. Chiyo. 1740. Called also Kansei. An expert of Tsuyama.

Kiuzō. Vide Mariyuki.

Kiuzui. Vide Hisayori.

Kiyohisa. Tanaka. 1860. Bunjiro; commonly called Fujiwara Bunjiro. An expert chiseller, celebrated for his skill in reproducing the works of the old masters. Yedo.

Kiyokaze. Fujii. 1700. Gembei. A pupil of the great Kaneko Yukinaka. Hagi.

Kiyonori. Goto. 1700. Rihei. Celebrated for making Kanto-tsubo; that is to say, guards ornamented with Chinese figures and landscapes. Yedo.

Kiyosada. Kusakari. 1790. Hachisaburo. Generally known as Kusakari Hachisaburo. Regarded as the greatest inlayer of Sendai. Celebrated for dragons (amaryo), landscapes, flowers, especially convolvulus, etc. Sendai.

Kiyosai. Vide Nagatake.

Kiyoshige. Tanaka. 1830. Minomatsu. Son of Kiyohisa and a skilled expert. Yedo.

Kiyoshige. Ito Katsumi (Vide). While still a pupil of Toriusai, was granted the art rank of Hokkyo, and used the mark Sciu Hokkyo Kiyoshige.

Kiyotaku. Inouye. 19th cent. Metal-worker of Yedo.

Kiyotoshi. Ito. 1840. A celebrated expert of Yedo. Art name, Juzo. Had rank of Hogen.

Kiyotsugu. Yoshioka. 1660. Had the title of Inaba-no-suke. Founded the Sendai branch of the Yoshioka family.

Kiyoyasu. Ito. 1750. Celebrated for inlaying in the Sumi-ye (sepia painting) style. Yedo.

Kiyoyori. Kusakari. 1830. Pupil of Teramitsu (Omori). Yedo and Sendai.

Kiyoyoshi. Goto. 1690. (Called also Seirei.) Common name, Shichibei. Kaga.

Kiyoyoshi. Goto. 1630. A pupil of Goto Seijo. Remarkably skilled in inlaying iron with gold, and in copying old masterpieces. Yedo.

Kiyoyoshi. Shiwamura. 1710. Celebrated as a maker of nanako. Yedo.

Kizayemon. 1700. Jakushi. A celebrated artist of Nagasaki. Like many of the Nagasaki experts, he affected figures taken from Chinese pictures (called "Canton style"or Kwanto-gata), but he also chiselled landscapes and seascapes with admirable effects of distance, dragons (the amaryo type), bamboos tossed by the wind, etc., with the greatest skill. He used his chisel so deftly that its trace resembles the brush strokes of a painter. His work has been largely imitated, and so well recognized is his tender, delicate, yet strong style, that the term "Jakushi" has come to be commonly applied to that class of carving. Nagasaki.

Koami. Kikuchi. 1650. Yagoro. A pupil of Goto Renjo, and an artist of the highest order. He combined the force and directness of the Goto style with the elaborateness of the Mito. Worked in Mito.

Kogitsune. 1670. A celebrated expert of Yechizen, famous for chiselling dragons.

Kogyosai. 19th cent. Art name also Gessan. Yedo.

Kōji. Yanagawa. 1860. A great expert of Kanazawa, pupil of Yanagawa Harushige. He died in 1877. Was commonly called Kanazawa Somin.

Kōjō. Goto. 1550. Fourth of the great Goto masters. Kyoto.

Kokusui. Wakabayashi. 1720. Rokubei. Toyama.

Komai. Matsuhiro. 19th cent. Yedo.

Komai. Otajiro. Present day. Metal-worker of Kyoto highly skilled in inlaying iron with gold by the Nunome process.

Komai. Seibei. 19th cent. Metal-worker of Higo, skilled in inlaying iron and sword furniture with gold. (d.1861).

Konju. Iwamoto. 1800. Kingoro. Yedo.

Konkwan. Iwamoto. 1770. Kisaburo. At first called Asai. A pupil of Riyokwan, and an expert of the highest merit. Celebrated for carving fish of various kinds, especially crustaceans, and for the beauty of his compositions. Used the marks Hakuhotei, Shunshodo, and Nampo, as well as his own name. Died, 1801. Yedo.

Konuki. Vide Masaharu.

Koreo. Ishiguro. 1840. A pupil of Koretsune. Called himself Hokuunsai. A skilled expert. Yedo.

Koreshige. Ishiguro. 1840. Ichiyo. A pupil of Koretsune. Yedo.

Koretsune. Ishiguro. 1840. Shukichi. Called himself Togakushi, Ritsumei, Shinryo, Hogiyokusai, Gishinken, Kounsai, and Ichiyeian. Second son of Masatsune (Ishiguro), the first, and an artist of superb skill. Yedo.

Koreyoshi. Ishiguro. 1850. Kwanjiro. Called himself Jikakushi and Kwansai. An expert of the highest skill. Yedo.

Koriusai. 19th cent. (d.1879). Metal-chiseller of Owari. Koriusai was his art name, his real name being Toyokawa Mitsunaga.

Koriusha. Vide Masahiro.

Koriyama. Mitsunaka. 19th cent. A metal-worker of Yedo.

Kōsen. Tanikawa. 1820. Chiuzayemon. Art name, Kounsai. Yedo.

Kosetsuken. Vide Tomonao.

Kōten. Supposed to have been a pupil of Aoki Jubei (q.v.). A skilled expert of Higo. He worked in the style of Kaneiye.

Kounsai. Vide Kosen.

Kounsai. Vide Koretsune.

Kozui. Vide Mitsuyori.

Kuhei. Inouye. 1750. Bunjiro. A pupil of Inouye Higeyasu. Commonly known as Sammonji-ya.

Kunichika. 19th cent. Metal-worker of Yedo.

Kuniharu. Tetsuya Dembei. Vide Harukuni.

Kunihiro. 1670. Kihei. Kaga.

Kunihiro. 1690. Yozayemon. Kaga.

Kunihisa. 1640. Jiuzayemon. A son of Kuninaga of Kaga.

Kunihisa. 1660. Jiuzayemon. A grandson of Kuninaga of Kaga.

Kunihisa. 1700. Yozayemon. Kaga.

Kunimasa. 1710. Yozayemon. Kaga.

Kuninaga. 1620. Jirosaku. A pupil of Goto Kakujo. He worked originally in Kyoto and moved to Kaga in 1620. His finest work was in inlaying. He is counted the earliest maker of inlaid sword-mounts in Kaga. His carving is known as Jiro-saku-bori.

Kuninaga. 1740. Yozayemon. Kaga.

Kuninaga. Uyemura. 1680. A skilled artist of Kyoto, generally known as Masuya Kuhei.

Kunishige. Miyochin. 1570. A great expert. Kozuke.

Kunitada. 1760. Gonzayemon. Kaga.

Kunitomo. Kobayashi. 1700. Date uncertain. A pupil of the Shoami experts in Kyoto.

Kuniyasu. Yozayemon. A pupil of Kuninaga Jirosaku. Kaga.

Kurokawa. Eisho. Present time. A Kinzoku-shi (metal-chiseller), celebrated for his skill in joining different metals to form a decorative design, and also for the Kiri-hame process (vide text), by means of which the artist produces plaques showing exactly the same decoration on face and back.

Kuwamura. Family name. Vide Hiroyoshi, etc.

Kuwamura. Yensuke. 19th cent. (d.1877). A skilled metal-chiseller of Kanazawa.

Kwaizantei. Vide Motomochi (Hiyama).

Kwakujusai. Vide Masahiro.

Kwanjō. Goto. 1640. Mitsunaga. Kyoto.

Kwanjō. Iwamoto. 1790. Shosuke or Shoshichi. Yedo.

Kwanju. Hamada. 1720. Toraizo. Art name, Gyokuriusai. A pupil of Joi, and a skilled expert. Shinshu.

Kwanri. Iwamoto. 1780. Kijiro. Called also Hirotoshi. Adopted son of Iwamoto Konkwan. Yedo. Art name, Jounsai.

Kwansai. Vide Koreyoshi.

Kwanzui. Vide Hiroyori.

Kwōrin. Otsuki. 1400. There is some uncertainty as to the date of this expert; but most authorities agree in placing him at the end of the fourteenth century. His work is excellent, though severe in style. Some of his pieces are marked "Nagoya no riyoshuku ni Kore wo tsukuru" (made in an inn in Nagoya).

Kwoyetsu. Fujimoto. 1660. Denjuro. A pupil of Goto Yetsujo. A skilled expert. Kaga.

Masaaki. Noda. 1820. Risuke. A skilled expert. Yedo.

Masachika. Tsuji. 1660. Genyemon. This artist came to Yedo in the year 1659, and four years afterwards was taken under the patronage of the Prince of Mito. He and his pupils and descendants worked thenceforth in Yedo. They were the younger branch of the Tsuji of Omi (vide Mitsumasa). Masachika did not mark his pieces, but the specimens attributed to him are very fine. He had no less than seven pupils, all of whom acquired some reputation; namely, Masanori, Masayuki, Masatoshi, Masamori, Masaoki, Masatomo, and Masataka.

Masachika. Tsuji. 1780. Gengoro. Grandson of the first Tsuji Masachika, used the mark Toun-sai. Yedo.

Masachika. Nara. 1760. Seiroku. He became a pupil of Joi and called himself Jowa. During two or three years after the death of his father, Masanaga, he used the latter's name on his works. He is not the peer of Masanaga, but nevertheless stands high.

Masachika. Ishiguro. 1840. Toyojiro. Yedo.

Masachika. Hirata. 1750. Ichizayemon. A pupil of Tsu Jimpo. Worked in Awa Province.

Masachika. Tsuchiya 1840. Art name, Sekiyenshi. An expert of fair skill. Yedo.

Masachika. Tsuchiya. 19th cent. Metal-worker of Yedo.

Masachika. Ito. 1760.

Matakichi. A Yedo expert, who carved in the Masatsune style.

Masafusa. Shimada. 1720. Shojiro. Toyama.

Masafusa. Shimada. 1660. Kenni Shojiro. A pupil of Morisada (Katsugi). A skilled expert. Toyama (Yetchiu).

Masafusa. Fujiki. 1670.

Masafusa. Shoami. 1570. An expert of Kameda (in Dewa).

Masafusa. Vide Masayuki (Tsuji).

Masaharu. Nomura. 1740. Kasuya Genshiro. Yedo.

Masaharu. 1750. Marked his pieces, Rinfudo. Family unknown and date uncertain. Yedo.

Masaharu. Tamagawa. 1800. Yuzo. Mito.

Masaharu. Tamagawa. 1840. Jugoro. Called himself Konuki. A skilled expert. Yedo.

Masahide. Ishiguro. 1840. Called Shogutei. Yedo.

Masahide. Nomura. 18th cent. Metal-worker of Hikone.

Masahide. Nomura. 1780. Hidegoro. Yedo.

Masahide. Nomura. 1770. Sadashiro. Pupil of Masatsugu (Nomura). Yedo.

Masahide. Nomura, 19th cent. Metal-worker of Yedo.

Masahira. 1730. Kanshichi, successor of Shigetsugu Kihachiro. Kaga.

Masahiro. Ichiguro. 1820. Matakichi. Called himself Gantoshi, Keiho, Kwakujusai, and Koriusha. A grand artist. Yedo.

Masahiro. Ito. 1850. An expert of Yedo.

Masahisa. Tamagawa. 1790. Bumpei. Mito.

Masakata. Ito. 1730. Genjiro. Son of Masatsune (Ito), and scarcely inferior to his father as an expert in carving à jour. Yedo and Bushiu.

Masakatsu. Minagawa. 1840. Genjiro. Yedo.

Masakatsu. Okada. 1740. Zenzayemon. Hagi.

Masakazu. Okamoto. 1730. Kohei. Hagi.

Masakazu. Tsuji. 1810. Genzo. Yedo.

Masakiyo. Ishiguro. 1830. Wasaburo. Called himself Jikiyopusai. A skilled expert of Yedo.

Masakiyo. Shoami. 1690. Worked at Wakamatsu in Aizu.

Masakuni. Nomura. 1770. Pupil of Masatsugu (Nomura). Yedo.

Masamichi. Nomura. 1730. Chotaku. Carver to the feudal chief of Awa. Tokushima.

Masamitsu. Nomura. 1760. Magoshichi. A pupil of Masatsugu. A celebrated expert. Yedo.

Masamitsu. Vide Yeijo.

Masamitsu. Kanedo. 1630. Kichi-no-jo. A celebrated Shitabori-shi, or preliminary chiseller who blocked out designs for the finishing expert. Kanazawa (Yedo).

Masamori. Hosono. 1600. Sozayemon, or Yoshimasa. An expert of Kyoto, celebrated for having been the first to develop the capabilities of Kebori-zogan or hair-line inlaying. His chiselling in relief is also very fine, and, on the whole, he belongs to the highest rank of artists.

Masanaga. Ito. 1700. Jingozayemon. Founder of the Ito family, which thenceforth enjoyed the distinction of making sword-guards for the Shoguns.

Masanaga. Tamagawa. 1780. Bumpei. Lived first in Mito (Hitachi) and afterwards in Yedo. A great expert, not inferior to his father Yoshinaga.

Masanaga. Ishiguro. 1840. Yeisuke. Yedo.

Masanaga. Nara. Shichirozayemon. 1730. A pupil of Toshinaga (Chikan). A celebrated expert. Yedo.

Masanaga. Nara. 1750. Pupil of Toshihisa. Used the mark Masaharu at first and afterwards that of Seiroku. An expert of the highest repute. His autumn landscapes, in which a mantis and eularia (suzuki) occupy the foreground, are celebrated for strength and delicacy.

Masanaga. Nara. 1740. Son of Masanaga, the first of the Nara family, but not so skilled as his father.

Masanaka. Nara. 1750. Pupil of Masachika. (Nara.) Yedo.

Masanaka. Kuwabara. 1750. Tokuzayemon. A pupil of Nara Masanaga. Yedo.

Masanaka. 19th cent. Metal-worker of Yedo. Art name, Hakushusai.

Masanao. Nomura. 18th and 19th cent. Metal-worker of Hikone.

Masanao. Shimada. 1740. Kensui Shodayu. A great expert. Toyama (Yetchiu).

Masanao. Nomura. 1720. Originally Wakabayashi Masagoro. A pupil of Masamitsu (Nomura). Yedo.

Masanari. Ito. 1820. An expert of Yedo.

Masanobu. Ito. 1680. Commonly called Tsuba-ya Tasuke, or " Tasuke, the guard maker." A skilled expert of Kyoto. Not a member of the Ito family proper.

Masanobu. Goto. 1630. Adopted by the painter Tanyu, and raised to the rank of Hokkyo in recognition of his excellence. Signed some of his work Toun. Kyoto.

Masanobu. 1750. Kambei. Son of Masahira Kanshichi. Kaga.

Masanobu. Nara. 1750. Zenji. Called himself Kikuju-sai, and Kiko. His first name was Masatsugu, then Masayuki. and finally Masanobu. A great expert, celebrated for his carvings of the Amariyo (a kind of dragon). Lived first in Yedo and afterwards in Osaka.

Masanobu. Shoami. 1620. Celebrated for having produced the eight views of Omi Lake on iron guards inlaid with gold. Kyoto.

Masanobu. Hamano. 1790. Tarobei. A skilled expert. Used four of Shozui's art names: Otsuriuken, Mibobu, Rifudo, and Kankyo.

Masanori. Ito. 1830. An expert of Yedo.

Masanori. Shoami. 1400. Ichirobei. Nothing certain is known of this artist, even his date being more or less speculative.

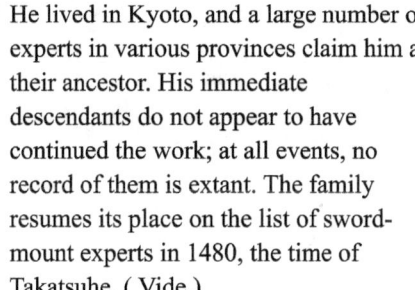

He lived in Kyoto, and a large number of experts in various provinces claim him as their ancestor. His immediate descendants do not appear to have continued the work; at all events, no record of them is extant. The family resumes its place on the list of sword-mount experts in 1480, the time of Takatsuhe. (Vide.)

Masanori. Murakumi. 1640. Tadushichi. Younger brother of the celebrated Jochiku, and a skilled carver and inlayer. Yedo.

Masanori. Hashibe. 1630. A pupil of Goto Teijo. Kyoto.

Masanori. Nomura. 1700. Shoyemon. Called also Itoku. A highly skilled artist. Yedo. Masanori. Okada. 1720. Hikozayemon. Nagato.

Masanori. Tsuji. 1680. Katsunosuke. Pupil of Tsuji Masachika (the first). Yedo.

Masanori. Tsuji. 1680. Pupil of Tsuji Masachika (the first). Called Jusaburo. Yedo.

Masanori. Nara. 1730. Pupil of the first Masanaga. He marked his works Masatsugu or Masayuki, as well as Masanori. Yedo.

Masaoki. Ishiguro. 1810. Sadakichi. Yedo.

Masaoki. Tsuji. 1680. Hamada Kiichi. Pupil of Tsuji Masachika (the first). Yedo.

Masasada. Takita. 1810. Seisuke. Mito.

Masasada. Hamano. 1740. Called also Masakazu. Personal name, Masazane. A pupil of Shozui.

Masashige. Shoami. 1650. A Kyoto expert, skilled in inlaying brass with silver, shakudo, etc.

Masashige. Nara. 1700. Pupil of Masachika (Nara). Yedo.

Masasuke. Tsuji. 1760. Mohachi. Yedo.

Masatada. Nomura. 1730. Shoyemon. Yedo.

Masataka. Okamoto. 1690. Sayemon. Called also Kozen. A skilled artist. Hagi.

Masataka. Tsuji. 1680. Gengoro. Pupil of Tsuji Masachika (the first). Yedo.

Masataka. Tsuji. 1790. Genyemon. Yedo.

Masatani. Ito. 1800. Matazk. An artist of Yedo.

Masatatsu. Wada. 1850. Art name, Gekendo. A highly skilled artist of Kyoto.

Masatatsu. Present day. A skilled metal-chiseller of Osaka.

Masatoki. Nomura. 1660. Kozayemon. The first of the Nomura family to attain distinction. Kyoto and Yedo.

Masatoki. Yamazaki. 1820. Ishimatsu. Art name, Seiseisai. Worked at Sukura in Shimosa.

Masatomi. Okada. 1760. Hikobei. Hagi.

Masatomo. Tsuji. 1680. Yamada. Masahachi. Pupil of Tsuji Masachika (the first). Yedo.

Masatomo. Tsuji. 1830. Genzo. Yedo.

Masatomo. Umetada. 1660. Hikobei. Hagi.

Masatomo. Ito. 1700. Yaiichi. Second son of Masanaga (Ito) Bushiu.

Masatomo. Okada. 18th cent. Metal-worker of Choshiu.

Masatoshi. Tsuji. 1680. Seijiro. Pupil of Tsuji Masachika (the first). Yedo.

Masatoshi. Ishiguro. 1810. Yasusuki. Yedo.

Masatoshi. Ito. 19th cent. Metal-worker of Yedo.

Masatoyo. Wada. 18th and 19th cent. Metal-worker of Yedo.

Masatoyo. Nomura. 1770. Pupil of Masamitsu (Nomura). Yedo.

Masatsugu. Shoami. 1720. Date uncertain. Kyoto.

Masatsugu. Umetada. 1700. A Kyoto expert, famous for inlaying shakudo with gold. He always marked his work "Yamashiro."

Masatsugu. Nomura. 1760. Magoshichi. His original family name was Nakamura. A great expert. Yedo.

Masatsugu. Vide Kenjo.

Masatsune. Nomura. 1800. Masagoro. A nanako expert. Yedo.

Masatsune. Ishiguro. 1780. Shusuke. Called himself Kimiyo, Togakushi and Jikokusai. He was also known as Koretsune. One of the greatest artists of modern times. Born 1759, died 1828. Celebrated for his bronze carvings as well as for his sword-mounts. Yedo.

Masatsune. Ishiguro. 1800. Taminosuke. Son of Togakushi, and nearly as great an artist as his father. Yedo. Art name, Keisai.

Masatsune. Ito. 1710. Jinyemon, or Jinzaburo. A celebrated Yedo expert, guard-maker to the Shoguns' Court. His decoration à jour is marvellously delicate, not inferior to that of the best Kinai work.

Masatsune. Igarashi. 1680. A skilled expert of Higo; supposed to have been the ninth in descent from Kaneiye. His art name was Tetsubaku.

Masatsune. 19th cent. Metal-worker of Yedo. Art name, Seisai.

Masaya. Nomura. 1700. Shoyemon. Called also Tomoyoshi or Yuki. A great expert, celebrated for his combination of metals forming the rare and beautiful mokume (wood-grain) grounds. He entered the service of the feudal chief of Awa and settled in Tokushima.

Masayasu. Ikagawa. 1800. Genshichi. He called himself Yoshodo. Celebrated for chiselling ornamental designs on the blades of swords. Mino.

Masayasu. Hirata. 1720. Yahachiro. A maker of iron guards inlaid with gold. Awa Province.

Masayori. Hamano. 1740. Tarobei. His name is generally pronounced Shozui. A pupil of the celebrated Nara Toshihisa, whose fame he rivals. He did not create a style of his own, but his work is strong, delicate, and full of artistic beauty. He called himself, Otsuruiken, Miboku, Kankyo, Rifudo Shijun, Yuko-tei, Shuhosai, Hankeishi, Isshunan, Gyokkeisha, and Keito. Worked in Yedo and died in 1769.

Masayori. Vide Hiyobu Hogen.

Masayoshi. Nomura. 1710. Kahiro. Called also Suihaku. Yedo.

Masayoshi. Nomura. 1790. Kotoji. Called also Ichiunsai. A great expert. Yedo.

Masayoshi. 1820. Isuke. A Samurai who became a pupil of Tomomasa Daishido. Yedo.

Masayoshi. Tsuchiya. 1770. Metal-worker of Yedo.

Masayoshi. Ishiguro. 1830. Shozo. Called himself Jikosai. A pupil of Jimiya, and a skilled expert. Yedo.

Masayoshi. Nara. 1750. Called commonly Shozui Bozu (the old man Shozui). A pupil of Masayori (Shozui), celebrated for imitating old works. Yedo.

Masayoshi. Ito. 1750. Jinyemon or Matakichiro. An expert of Yedo, grandson of Masatsune (Ito).

Masayoshi. Nomura, 19th cent. Metal-worker of Yedo.

Masayuki. Nomura. 1710. Shojiro. Called also Riyoyen. Yedo.

Masayuki (sometimes called Masafusa). Tsuji. 1680. Shojiro. Pupil of Tsuji Masachika (the first). Yedo. He founded a branch family, that of Fujiki, and took the name of Fujiki-kohachi.

Afterwards he called himself Ryoyei.

Masuya. Kuhei. Vide Kuninaga.

Masuya. Kichibei. Vide Kichibei.

Masuya. Yohei. Vide Yohei.

Masuya. Uhei. Vide Jokwo.

Masuya. } Vide Jochiku.
Bunyemon. } Vide Jochiku.

Masuya. Kuyemon (or Kihei). Vide Munemine.

Matabei. Muneta. 1540. There were three of this name in the family. The second (1560) is celebrated as the first maker of Go-no-me nanako. The third used the mark Doi. Vide also, Norinao and Naomichi. Kyoto.

Matashichi. Muneta. 1560. Vide also, Naoshige. Kyoto.

Matashichi. Shoami. 1700. The date is uncertain. An expert of Chikuzen.

Matazayemon. Muneta. 1520. There were three of this name. The second Matazayemon (1560), and the third (1600). The last sometimes used the mark Dosei. Kyoto.

Matsumoto. Kanjiro. Present day. One of the pioneers of the school of modern craftsmen who have carried to a high pitch of excellence the art of inlaying iron, bronze, shibuichi, and shakudo with gold and silver. Works in Tokyo.

Matsumura. Shoami. 1850. Bunyemon. An expert of Aizu.

Meiju. Umetada Okada. 1640. Originally an artist of Kyoto, but moved to Hagi in Choshiu, and founded the Okada family of that place (vide Nobumasa).

Meishin. Vide Shigeyoshi Umetada.

Miboku. Vide Masayori and Kaneyori, Norinobu and Masanobu.

Minjo. 19th cent. (d.1864). A great metal-chiseller of Yedo.

Minkoku. 19th cent. A great metal-chiseller of Tokyo, who worked in conjunction with Shuraku, Temmin, Riumin, and Minjo, forming the goningumi (five men company), who produced many splendid works between 1854 and 1860. Minkoku is now too old to work.

Minriu. 18th and 19th cent. Great metal-worker of (Tokyo) Yedo.

Mitane. Shigeyoshi. 19th cent. Metal-worker of Yedo.

Mitsu. The second ideograph of this name is disguised, and cannot be read, nor has it been identified as the mark of any expert. The name is found, however, on very beautiful rings and tips of shakudo, with finely polished ground, delicate decoration of herons, river scenes, etc. Probable date, 1730.

Mitsuaki. Goto. 1850. Sixteenth representative of the Goto family. Called Hojo. Yedo.

Mitsuaki. Ishiguro. 1850. Tetsugoro. Yedo.

Mitsuaki. Goto. 1570. Jinyemon. Kaga.

Mitsuchika. Vide Reijo.

Mitsuchika. Vide Joyo.

Mitsufusa. Hayata. 1830. Zennosuke. A pupil of Terumitsu (Omori). Hirado (Hizen).

Mitsufusa. Yatobe. Tamagawa. 1790. Hikoroku. A celebrated artist of Mito. His name is commonly pronounced Tsuju. Father of the great Yoshinaga of Mito.

Mitsuharu. Goto. 1670. Kyoto.

Mitsuharu. Vide Yekijo.

Mitsuharu. Goto. 1710. Commonly called Kambei. Kyoto.

Mitsuhaya. Shoami. 1810. A guard-maker of Kyoto.

Mitsuhide. Vide Yenjo.

Mitsuhiro. Goto. 1700. Kyoto.

Mitsuhisa. Vide Taijo.

Mitsuhisa. Vide Genyemon.

Mitsuhisa. Yatabe. 1740. Hikoroku. A skilled expert of Mito, pupil of Koami.

Mitsukata. 19th cent. Metal-worker of Choshiu.

Mitsukatsu. Vide Kaijo.

Mitsukuni. Vide Yetsujo.

Mitsukyo. Vide Senjo.

Mitsumasa. Vide Shoyo.

Mitsumasa. Goto. 1620. One of the three Mino-bori (vide Kakujo). Mino.

Mitsumasa. Goto. 1720. The twelfth Goto Master. Kyoto.

Mitsumasa. Vide Teijo.

Mitsumasa. Mizuno. 1660. Genroku. Kaga.

Mitsumasa. Kikuoka. 1770. Brother of Mitsuyuki Kikuoka.

Mitsumasa. Tsuji. 1750. Tanji. Called himself Rinsendo. An expert of the highest rank, skilled in every kind of work, takabori, kebori, zogan, etc. His work is compared by Japanese connoisseurs to a spray of plum-blossom in a beautiful vase. He worked chiefly in Omi province, but lived for some time in Yedo with Soyo. He died in 1776, at the age of 53.

Mitsumichi. Ishiguro. 1810. Sanjiro. A pupil of Jimiyo. Yedo.

Mitsumori. Goto. 1760. The fourteenth Goto Master. Called Keijo. Yedo.

Mitsunaga. Vide Kwanjo.

Mitsunaga. Vide Shunjo.

Mitsunaga. Vide Seijo.

Mitsunami. Goto. 1690. Kyoto.

Mitsunari. Goto. 1600. Kihei. Vide Zenjo. Kyoto.

Mitsunobu. Goto. 1690. Kyoto.

Mitsunobu. Vide Kakujo.

Mitsunobu. Miyagawa. 1830. Kichijo. A pupil of Terumitsu (Omori). Yedo.

Mitsunori. Goto. 1860. Seventeenth representative of the Goto family. Called Tenjo. Died 1879. The last of the Goto experts. Yedo.

Mitsunori. Goto. 1760. Kyoto.

Mitsunori. Goto. 1680. Kyoto.

Mitsunori. Vide Keijo.

Mitsunori. Goto. 1670. Kyoto.

Mitsunori. Vide Joren.

Mitsunori. Vide Zenjo.

Mitsuoki. Goto. 1680. Kyoto.

Mitsusada. Vide Renjo.

Mitsusada. Murakami. 1750. Todayu. Toyama.

Mitsusada. 1720. Iyemon. A pupil of Somin.

Mitsusato. Goto. 1610. One of the three Mino-bori (vide Kakujo). Celebrated for deeply chiselled landscapes. Mino.

Mitsusato. 19th cent. Metal-worker of Yedo.

Mitsushige. Vide Sokujo.

Mitsushima. Goto. 1660. Shichizayemon. Kyoto.

Mitsushiro. Otsuki. 19th cent. Metal-worker of Yedo.

Mitsusuke. Goto. 1670. Kyoto.

Mitsutada. Goto. 1610. Kyoto.

Mitsutada. Vide Kiujo.

Mitsutaka. Vide Yenjo.

Mitsutaka. Saito. 1830. Ginzo. Pupil of Teramitsu (Omori). Sendai.

Mitsutaka. Morimura. 1840. A highly skilled expert of Yedo. Celebrated for chiselling insects.

Mitsutaka. Vide Shujo.

Mitsutake. Goto. 1640. Kyoto.

Mitsutaki. Kikuoka. 19th cent. Metal-worker of Yedo. Art name, Kinkodo.

Mitsutatsu. 19th cent. Metal-worker of Yedo. Art name, Ichijiu-sai.

Mitsutatsu. Omori. 19th cent. Metal-worker of Yedo.

Mitsuteru. Mikami. 1730. A pupil of Yanagawa Naomitsu. Yedo.

Mitsutoki. Kakinuma. 1830. Shinzo. A pupil of Terumitsu (Omori). Yedo.

Mitsutomi. Vide Injo.

Mitsutomo. Vide Renjo.

Mitsutomo. Goto. 1720. Rihei. Kyoto.

Mitsutomo. 19th cent. Metal-worker of Yedo.

Mitsutoshi. Vide Kwanjo.

Mitsutoshi. Kikuoka. 19th cent. Metal-worker of Yedo.

Mitsutoshi. Vide Tsojo.

Mitsutoyo. Vide Shujo.

Mitsutoyo. Vide Shujo and Kambei.

Mitsutsugu. Yoshioka. 1740. Kayemon or Munehiro. Yedo.

Mitsutsuke. Goto. 1760. Kyoto.

Mitsutsuna. Vide Kaijo.

Mitsutsune. Otsuki. 1750. Yamashiro-ya Kihachi. Said to be the nineteenth in descent from Kworin. Kyoto.

Mitsutsune. Nakai. 1590. Founder of the well known family of Hagi (vide Nobutsune) guard-makers. Frequently used the mark Jokan Inshi. Suwo.

Mitsutsune. Nakai. 1390. The founder of the Nakai family. He worked at Suwo in Yamaguchi, and his art name was Sakan Inshi.

Mitsuyori. Vide Ritsujo.

Mitsuyori. Murata. 1760. Hanjiro. Called also Kozui. Used the mark Ichiyodo. Yedo.

Mitsuyoshi. Goto. 1830. Fifteenth representative of the Goto family. Called Shinjo. Yedo. Art name, Shintoken.

Mitsuyoshi. Nishimura. 1750. Sasaya Genzuki. A good expert pupil of Mitsutsune (Otsuki). Kyoto.

Mitsuyoshi. Vide Joken.

Mitsuyoshi. Vide Genjo.

Mitsuyoshi. Tachibana. 1840. A skilled expert of Yedo. Art name, Shojo, indicating his love of wine.

Mitsuyuki. Vide Unjo.

Mitsuyuki. Kikuoka. 1760. Ritoji. Called himself Dopposai and Saika-an, which names are found on his works. A pupil of Yanagawa Naomitsu, and an expert of the highest order. He carved in the Yokoya style, and Japanese connoisseurs, speaking of the delicacy and strength of his chiselling, say that it resembles feather-grass drooping heavy with dew, but not touching the ground. Yedo.

Mitsuyuki. Goto. 1680. Kyoto.

Mitsuzane. Vide Rinjo.

Miyasaka. Yoshimasa. Present day. Metal-sculptor. Pupil of Unno Shomin.

Miyōchin. Family of armourers and workers in metal. The genealogy of the family extends back to the second century of the Christian era, but as armourers their history may be said to commence with the sixteenth representative, Munemichi. The names are as follows, in chronological order:

Miyōchin. Munemichi. 640 A.D.

Miyōchin. Munetsugu. 670. Said to have forged armour for the Emperor Tenji.

Miyōchin. Munetoshi. 690.

Miyōchin. Munematsu. 720.

Miyōchin. MunemorL 760.

Miyōchin. Munemaro. 800. Armourer to the Emperor Kwamma and Seiwa.

Miyōchin. Muneshima. 820.

Miyōchin. Munekuni. 840.

Miyōchin. Munetora, 860.

Miyōchin. Muneyori. 880.

Miyōchin. Muneshimo. 890.

Miyōchin. Munemori. 910.

Miyōchin. Munetoshi. 930.

Miyōchin. Munezane. 980. Said to have forged a shield of gold for Minamoto no Mitsunaka.

Miyōchin. Munekazu. 1010.

Miyōchin. Munekuni. 1030.

Miyōchin. Munenaka. 1060.

Miyōchin. Munetsune. 1100. Known in the artistic world as Go-Munetsugu, or the "second Munetsugu," having changed his name to Munetsugu in his late years. Said to have forged iron armour decorated with eight varieties of dragons (hachi-riyo).

Miyōchin. Muneyoshi. 1140.

Miyōchin. Munesuke (1). 1154 to 1185. Called also Masuda. Had the rank of Idzumo no Kami. Worked first in Idzumo for Yoritomo; then in Kyoto, and finally for the Minamoto in Kamakura. He is said to have forged the suit of armour worn by Yoshitsume, and now preserved at the Kasuga Temple. Commonly he is spoken of as the first representative of the family, but the fact is that the art of decorative forging first became admirable in his hands.

Miyōchin. Munekiyo (2). 1200. Worked at Kamakura. Had the rank of Giyobu Taiyu.

Miyōchin. Muneyuki (3). 1215. Worked at Kyoto. Had rank of Giyobu Taiyu.

Miyōchin. Munemasu (4). 1225. Worked at Katsuyama in the province of Kii. One of the greatest of the Miyochin artists. Had the rank of Hyoye-no-Suke.

Miyōchin. Muneyoshi. 1200. Second son of Munesuke.

Miyōchin. Munehide. 1200. Third son of Munesuke.

Miyōchin. Muneyasu. 1200. Fourth son of Munesuke.

Miyōchin. Yoshikiyo. 1220. Son of Muneyoshi.

Miyōchin. Yoshitsugu. 1220. Son of Muneyoshi.

Miyōchin. Munenao. 1230. Second son of Munekiyo.

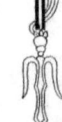

Miyōchin. Muneshige (5). 1240. Lived at Odawara. Had the rank of Sakyo no Tayu.

Miyōchin. Munekane. 1240. Second son of Muneyuki.

Miyōchin. Munesumi. 1250. Third son of Muneyuki.

Miyōchin. Muneto. 1240. Second son of Munemasu.

Miyōchin. Munetada (6). 1270. Worked at Sano in Mino. Had the rank of Shin-dayu.

Miyōchin. Shigeiye. 1270. Second son of Muneshige.

Miyōchin. Yoshishige. 1270. Third son of Muneshige.

Miyōchin. Munetsuna (7). 1300. Worked in Kyoto. Had rank of Sakon no Tayu.

Miyōchin. Muneyoshi. 1310. Second son of Munetada.

Miyōchin. Munemitsu (8). 1320. Worked in Kyoto. Had rank of Hyobu Taiyu.

Miyōchin. Munenori. 1330. Second son of Munetsuna.

Miyōchin. Munemasa (9). 1330. Worked in Kyoto. Had rank of Sakon no Tayu.

Miyōchin. Muneyasu (10). 1380. Worked in Kyoto. Had rank of Hyoye-no-Suke. Made a gold helmet for the Shogun Yoshimitsu. He received large estates in recognition of his skill. The first ten generations of the family, from Munesuke in the twelfth century to Muneyasu in the fourteenth, are known as "Miyōchin no Judai," or the "Ten generations of Miyōchin." They occupy in the history of armour-forging a place somewhat analogous to that occupied by the fourteen generations of Goto masters in the history of sword-mount decoration. Muneyasu, the tenth representative, is specially celebrated.

Miyōchin. Munetoki. 1380. Second son of Munemasa.

Miyōchin. Yoshihiro (11). 1400. Worked in Kyoto. Had rank of Sakyo no Tayu.

Miyōchin. Yoshitada (12). 1420. Worked in Kyoto. Rank, Sahiyoye no Jo.

Miyōchin. Yoshinori (13). 1440. Worked in Kyoto. Called also Gorodayu.

Miyōchin. Yoshinaga (14). 1450. Worked in Kyoto. Rank, Shikibu Tayu. One of the greatest of the family.

Miyōchin. Yoshiari (15). 1480. Worked at Kamakura. Called also Shinjiro.

Miyōchin. Yoshiyasu (16). 1520. Worked at Fuchiu in Hitachi and at Odawara. Called also Samuro-dayu. The six representatives from (11) to (16) are known as the Rokudai, or the " Six Generations." They are also called Giyoshi, or the "Honourable Masters." The names are : Yoshihiro, Yoshitada, Yoshinori, Yoshinaga, Yoshiari, and Yoshiyasu.

Miyōchin. * Takayoshi. 1450. Second son of Yoshinori, and not a representative of the main line, but one of the most celebrated of the Miyochin artists. Worked at Kamakura.

Miyōchin. Yoshihisa. 1460. Second son of Yoshinaga.

Miyōchin. * Yoshimichi. 1500. Second son of Yoshiari. Worked in Kyoto. Not a representative of the main line, but a renowned master.

Miyōchin. Katsuyoshi. 1510. Third son of Yoshiari.

Miyōchin. * Nobuiye (17). 1520. Originally called Yasuiye. Worked at Shirai in Joshiu. One of the most celebrated of the Miyochin Masters. The three names marked with an asterisk, Takayoshi, Yoshimichi, and Nobuiye are those of the "Nochi no Sansaku," or "Three Later Masters."

Miyōchin. Narikuni. 1470. Worked at Yawata in Joshiu. Son of Yoshihisa.

Miyōchin. Kunichika. 1420. Son of Yoshihisa.

Miyōchin. Narichika. 1420. Son of Yoshihisa. Worked in Joshiu. One of the great Miyochin Masters.

Miyōchin. Narishige. 1500. Son of Narichika. Worked at Yawata in Kozuke. One of the great Miyochin Masters.

Miyōchin. Kunihisa. 1530. Son of Narishige.

Miyōchin. Hisaiye. 1550. Son of Kunihisa. Worked at Kamakura. One of the Miyochin celebrities.

Miyōchin. Fusanobu. 1530. Son of Yoshiyasu.

Miyōchin. Munehisa. 1580. Grandson of Yoshiyasu.

Miyōchin. Katsumasa. 1580. Grandson of Yoshiyasu. Worked in Joshiu. One of the great Miyochin Masters.

Miyōchin. Yoshihisa. 1630. Son of Munehisa. Worked at Kamakura. One of the great Miyochin Masters.

Miyōchin. Yoshishige. 1620. Son of Yoshihisa.

Miyōchin. Sadaiye (18). 1550. Worked in Odawara and Iga. Called also Hachiro and Heiroku.

Miyōchin. Fusaiye. 1540. Second son of Nobuiye. Worked in Joshiu. A great master.

Miyōchin. Fusamune. 1550. Third son of Nobuiye. Worked at Odawara. A celebrity.

Miyōchin. Muneiye (19). 1580. Worked in Omi. Manufactured a celebrated helmet for Tokugawa Iyeyasu. Called also Kindaro.

Miyōchin. Munenobu (20). 1600. Son of Muneiye. Worked in Yedo and Osaka. One of the great Miyochin Masters.

Miyōchin. Munekiyo. 1620. Second son of Muneiye.

Miyōchin. Munenaga. 1620. Third son of Muneiye.

Miyōchin. Kunimori (21). 1620. Worked in Yedo. Son of Munenobu. Had rank of Nagato no Kami. Called also Kunimichi.

Miyōchin. Harunobu. 1620. Second son of Munenobu.

Miyōchin. Muneshige (22). 1640. Worked in Yedo. Had rank of Nagato no Kami.

Miyōchin. Munetoshi or Kunimichi. (23), 1650. Worked in Yedo.

Miyōchin. Munenushi. 1650. Second son of Muneshige.

Miyōchin. Munemasa. 1650. Third son of Muneshige.

Miyōchin. Munesuke (24). 1710. Worked in Yedo. Had rank of Osumi no Kami.

Miyōchin. Munemasa (25). 1730. Second son of Munesuke. Worked in Yedo, and had rank of Osumi no Kami.

Miyōchin. Munemasa (26). 1740. Worked in Yedo. Had rank of Nagato no Kami. Called also Seijiro.

Miyōchin. Munetaye (27). 1760. Had rank of Osumi no Kami.

Miyōchin. Pupils of Yoshimichi. 1500. Kyoto.

1. Yoshikatsu.
2. Yoshimichi.
3. Yoshiiye.

Miyōchin. Pupils of Nobuiye. 1520. Joshiu.

1. Iyefusa.
2. Nobutada.
3. Nobuyuki.
4. Nobumasa.
5. Nobutsuna.
6. Nobumitsu.

Miyōchin. Pupils of Narishige. 1500. Kozuke.

1. Nariyoshi
2. Naritada.
3. Naritsugu.
4. Munehisa.
5. Munetoki.

Mioju. Vide Shigeyoshi Umetada (Hikujiro).

Mizuno. Family name. Vide Yoshishige.

Mizuno. Gesshiu. Present day. A skilled sculptor in metal. Pupil of Unno Shomin.

Mogarashi. Vide Sōden. (Ed. Sōten)

Mori. Joken. 19th cent. Metal-worker of Tokyo. Also skilled as a wood-carver.

Moriaki. Ishiguro. 1820. Torajiro. Yedo.

Moriakira. Kuwamura. 1640. Jihei. A great expert. Son of Morihiro. Kaga.

Morichika. Inouye. 1860. A skilled expert of Tokyo. Pupil of Arichika.

Morihira. Katsugi. 1720. Iyemon. Kaga.

Morihiro. Kuwamura. 1620. Jihei. Art name, Riyoyu. A skilled expert, not inferior to his brother Morikatsu. Kaga.

Morikata. Yoshishige. 1690. Genshiro. Kaga.

Morikatsu. Kuwamura. 1620. Matsushiro, and afterwards Choyemon. A celebrated carver. Art name, Riyoyu. Kaga.

Morikatsu. Murata. 1780. A pupil of the Shoami family of Iyo. Used the mark Murata Ro, or the "old man Murata."

Morikuni. Katsugi. 1740. Tozayemon. Kaga.

Morikuni. Katsugi. 1770. Tozayemon. Some very beautiful iron guards by this expert are in existence. Kaga.

Morikuni. Shoami. 1730. Sosho. A great master in carving dragons and clouds.

Matsuyama (Iyo). Marked his work Shoami Sosho.

Morimichi. Kuwamura. 1660. Zenji. A celebrated expert, not inferior to his brother Moriyuki. Kaga.

Morimichi. Sato. 1810. Yaichiro. Mito.

Morimine. Shoami. 1600. Founded the Iyo branch of the Shoami family, and is therefore sometimes spoken of as the "Second Founder" of the family (vide Takatsune and Norisada). Worked at Matsuyama.

Morimine. Shoami. 1640. Worked at Matsuyama in Iyo.

Morimitsu. Katsugi. 1650. Hachibei. A pupil of Morisada Hanshiro. Kaga.

Morimitsu. Kuwamura. 1660. Kinshiro. A good carver. Pupil of Koko. Kaga.

Morimitsu. Katsugi. 1680. Kanyemon. A skilled expert: at first an inlayer, and afterwards a carver. Worked originally in Kaga, and then entered the service of the feudal chief of Toyama.

Morimura. Yukimori. 19th cent. Metal-worker of Yedo.

Morisada. Katsugi. 1690. Yoshiro, and afterwards Hanshiro. A skilled artist; grandson of Morisada Yozayemon. He entered the service of the feudal chief of Toyama. His son of the same name (Hanshiro) succeeded him. There were thus four Morisadas of the Katsugi family.

Morisada. Katsugi. 1640. Yozayemon. A highly skilled artist. He worked first in Fushimi and afterwards entered the service of the feudal chief of Kaga, receiving an annual allowance of fifty bags of rice.

Morisada. Katsugi. 1660. Yoshiro. Son of Morisada Yozayemon and counted of equal skill with his father. His son, of the same personal name, succeeded him. Kaga.

Morishige. Kuwamura. 1640. Seishiro. Kaga.

Moritsugu. Vide Soyo.

Moritsugu. Katsugi. 1690. Genzayemon. Kaga.

Moriyoshi. Katsugi. 1670. Sozayemon. Kaga.

Moriyoshi. Kuwamura. 1610. Yoshiro. The founder of the Kuwamura family.

Moriyuki. Kuwamura. 1640. Jirosaburo. A very celebrated artist. Kaga.

Motoaki. Morioka. 1800. Heizaburo. Pupil of Kaizantei. Mito.

Motoakira. Suzuki. 1780. Shinsuke. Called himself Tankasai. A great expert. Pupil of Sekijoken. Mito.

Motochika. Hiyama. 1780. Hanroku. Called himself Kaizantei. A skilled expert. Pupil of Sekijoken. Mito.

Motochika. Fujita. 1800. Jisaku. Called himself Ontaiken. A skilled expert. Mito.

Motoharu. Katoji. 1780. Jiyemon. Called himself Genjuken. Pupil of Sekijoken and a great expert. Mito.

Motohide. Sato. 1830. Gensuke. A pupil of Seiunsai. Mito.

Motohiro. Shimizu. 1800. Yeikichi. Mito.

Motohiro. 1780. Shinzaburo. Pupil of Sekijoken. Mito.

Motohisa. Nakamura. 1810. Magoshichi. Mito.

Motohisa. Yoshikawa. 1800. Yogoro. Called himself Tokaken. A pupil of Chikuzanken and a skilled expert. Mito.

Motokore. Ishikawa. 1780. Shoyemon. Mito.

Motokyo. 19th cent. Metal-worker of Yedo.

Motomichi. Yasuyama. 1790. Kinjiro. Mito.

Motomitsu. Gunji. 1800. Sozaburo. Pupil of Kaizantei. Mito.

Motomochi. Hiyama. 1810. Nihei. Called himself Kwaizantei. A skilled expert. Mito.

Motonaga. Nanjo. 1780. Shinzaburo. Pupil of Sekijoken. Mito.

Motonaga. Yamamoto. 1800. Shikohachi. Pupil of Kinzantei. Mito.

Motonaga. Ogawa. 1800. Chingoro. Called himself Jichikaken. A skilled expert. Mito.

Motonobu. Hanawa. 1780. Shinzo. Mito.

Motonobu. Watanabe. 1810. Tsunekichi. A pupil of Ontaiken. Mito.

Motonori. Kurozawa. 1810. Ichijiro. A pupil of Tohoken. Mito.

Motonori. Nemoto. 1800. Shinraku. Called himself Chooken. A skilled expert. Mito.

Motonori. Onose. 1780. Shinraku. Pupil of Sekijoken. Mito.

Motonori. Yasuyama. 1700. Shinsuke. Called himself Hozanken. Originally of the Yokoya family. A pupil of Chobei (Kikugawa), and, like his teacher, famous for carving chrysanthemums. Father of Seke-Joken. Mito.

Motosada. Ogawa. 1780. Shingoro. Called himself Chikuzanken. A pupil of Sekijoken. Mito.

Motosada. Tani. 19th cent. Metal-worker of Osaka.

Motoshige. Sakamoto. 1780. Genzaburo. Mito.

Motoshige. Mimura. 1810. Juzaburo. Called himself Seiunsai. A skilled expert. Mito.

Motoshige. Ogawa. 1800. Genji. Mito.

Mototaka. Nagayama. 1810. Motohachi. A pupil of Tohoken. Mito.

Mototaka. 1810. A pupil of Jichikuken. Mito.

Mototera. Yasuyama. 1780. Yeisuke. Mito.

Mototomo. 1780. Joi. Called himself Seishinken. A skilled expert. Mito.

Mototoshi. Yamagata. 1820. A Mito expert. A pupil of Seishinken.

Mototsune. Gunji. 1780. Shimpachi. Mito.

Motoyama. Munehide. 19th cent. Metal-worker of Yedo.

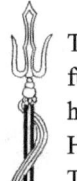

Motoyasu. Uchikishi. 1800. Shobei. Pupil of Kaizantei. Mito.

Motoyasu. Yasuyama. 1790. Yasujiro. Mito

Motoyori. Hida. 1810. Ichijiro. A pupil of Tohoken. Mito.

Motoyoshi. Yamagata. 1810. A pupil of Tohoken. Mito.

Motoyoshi. Sasaki. 1780. Chiuji. Pupil of Sekijoken. Mito.

Motoyuki. Watahiro. 1780. Hikosaburo. Mito.

Motoyuki. Suzuga. 1800. Gensuke. Pupil of Tankusai. Mito.

Motozumi. Yasuyama. 1760. Shinzayemon. Also called Sekijoken, and afterwards Togu. An artist of the highest skill, celebrated for chiselling figures in Chinese and Japanese style in shibuichi. He also carved mountain genii (sennin) with grand power and delicacy in the style of Joi. It is on record that he copied many of the old masterpieces. Lived in Mito, but often visited Yedo. Died at the age of 90 (1791), and worked vigorously on his 88th birthday. His son Tozaburo (also called Shinyemon) carved in the same style but with inferior ability. Mito.

Mukai. Shoko. Present day. An expert sculptor in metal. Pupil of Unno Shomin.

Muneaki. Nomura. 1730. Sokuro. Art name, Jumeishi. Hikone.

Muneaki. Nomura. 1730. His name is also pronounced Soken. Called also Yumeishi. A pupil of Kanenori (Nomura). Worked at Hikone.

Munechika. Miyochin. 18th cent. Metalworker of Matsuye (in Haruta).

Munechika. Tachibana and Fujiwara. 1000. At first called Nakamune. The founder of the Umetada family. A nobleman who employed his leisure in forging swords, and thus came to be called Sanjo no Kokaji (the amateur forger of Sanjo).

There is no evidence that he made sword-furniture, but he is included in this list as he founded one of the families of repute. He was born in 960 and died in 1030. The name Umetada was not adopted until the nineteenth generation after Munechika, namely, the time of Shigemune.

Munefusa. Fujita. 1650. Date uncertain. Younger brother of Fujita Munehisa and a skilled expert. Kaga.

Munehiro. Vide Sokwan.

Munehisa. Fujita. 1640. Date uncertain. Danyemon. A skilled expert. Younger brother of Umetada Nobufusa. Kaga.

Munehisa. Soami. 1650. Yumeishi. A pupil of Soden. (Ed. Soten) Worked at Hikone.

Munemasa. 1710. Kaheiji. A pupil of Somin. Carver to Matsudaira, feudal chief of Hizen.

Munemasa. Inouye. 1650. Kyoto.

Munemime. Uyemura. 1720. Kuyemon or Kihei. A great expert. Called also Soho, and commonly Masuya Kihei. Renowned for carving warriors. Kyoto.

Munemochi. Alternative pronunciation of Soyu. Vide Toshiharu (Nara).

Munenaga. 1690. Kuroji. Son of Munetsugu Jiro. Kaga.

Munenori. 1770. Bennosuke. A pupil of Tetsuya Gembei. Kyoto.

Munenori. Miyochin. 1540. A maker of guards. He was remarkably skilled in tempering iron. His guards generally have, on the face, Tosa no Kuni-ju Miyochin Munenori (Miyochin Munenori residing in Tosa), and on the reverse, Shinto Gotesuren (five times wrought iron, Shinto).

Munenori. Alternative pronunciation of Soden (q.v.) (Ed. Soten).

Munenori. Vide Nobutsugu.

Munenori. 1770. Bennosuke. A pupil of Tetsuya Gembei. Kyoto.

Munesuke. Ki. 1640. Known as Miyochin Osumi no Kami (Miyochin Lord of Osumi). A descendant of Nobuiye and a skilled expert. Yedo.

Muneto. Family name. Vide Naomichi.

Munetoki. Umetada. 1830. Shichizayemon. Representative of the thirty-fifth generation of the Umetada family. Worked in Yedo.

Munetoshi. Nara. 1720. Son of Toshinaga, fourth representative of the Nara family.

Munetsugu. 1670. Jiro; son of Muneyoshi Hiyobu. Kaga.

Munetsugu. Yoshioka. 1690. Chojiro, or Choyemon. Afterwards called Sokei. Yedo.

Munetsugu. Yoshioka. 1820. Bungon. Yedo.

Muneyoshi. 1650. Hiyobu. Went from Fushimi to Kaga in the year 1645. A great expert. Received an allowance of one hundred bags of rice yearly from the feudal chief of Kaga.

Muneyoshi. Umetada. 1670. Munetaka. Date uncertain. He had the title of Kazuma-no-suke and lived in Osaka. His work, which is of high quality, carried the inscription, Tachibana Muneyoshi.

Muneyuki. Umetada. 1640. Representative of the twenty-eighth generation of the Umetada family. Celebrated for chiselling guards with pierced decoration. He worked for the Tokugawa Court in the time of the third Shogun, Iyemitsu, but resided in Kyoto. By him the first ideograph of the name Umetada was changed from Ume (to bury) to Ume (Plum), and the Umetada artists thenceforth marked their pieces with a plum blossom above the ideograph Tada. The representatives of the family worked during thirty-six generations, and their record was compiled in 1830 by Munetoki, the 35th.

Muneyuki. 18th and 19th cent. Metalworker of Yedo. Art name, Kiriusai.

Nagaatsu. Suga. 1720. A pupil of Narikado (Hirata) and a skilled expert in enamel decoration. Yedo.

Nagafusa. Hirata. 1760. Ichizayemon. A pupil of Masatsugu (Nomura). Worked in Awa.

Nagafusa. Hirata. 1760. Ichizayemon. Takashima. (Awa.)

Nagahide. Hirata, 1770. Shingo. Worked in Awa.

Nagahisa. 1650. Shichibei. Kaga.

Nagahisa. 1660. Genzayemon. Kaga.

Nagakiyo. 1720. Kanroku. Kaga.

Nagakiyo. Tazawa. 1620. Original family name Katsugi, changed it subsequently to Tazawa, and received a yearly salary from the feudal chief of Kaga as a skilled expert.

Nagakuni. Koichi. 1700. Yazayemon. Kaga.

Nagamasa. Koichi. 1650. Saburoyemon. An expert in inlaying. Kaga.

Nagamine. 1730. Jirozo. A grand artist, celebrated for his fine chiselling of men in armour, the figures full of life and motion, and even the faces animated. His father of the same name was also a good expert. Kyoto.

Nagamitsu. 1760. Hambei. Kaga.

Naganobu. 1670. Rokuyemon. Kaga.

Naganobu. 1680. Kichidayu. Kaga.

Nagasada. 1730. Jisuke. Kaga.

Nagasone. Akao. 1800. Saichi. A guardmaker who worked in the Akao style, but used iron approximating to steel. Yedo.

Nagashige. 1720. Kuroyemon; successor of Munenaga Kuroji. Kaga.

Nagashige. Koichi. 1650. Shirazaburo. An inlayer and carver of Kaga.

Nagatake. Imai. 1850. Art name, Kyosui. Kyoto expert of great skill.

Nagatsugu. Shoami. 1600. Yoshiro. Said to have been the first to inlay brass with gold, silver, shakudo, etc. Hence such work is commonly known as the "Yoshiro style" (Yoshiro-fu). Worked at Mino.

Nagatsugu. Yoshioka. 1640. Chozaburo. Yedo.

Nagatsugu. 1780. Toyotsugu. Kaga.

Nagatsugu. Koichi. 1760. Yazayemon. Kaga.

Nagatsugu. Koichi. 1740. Yazayemon. Kaga.

Nagatsugu. Koichi. 1670. Yazayemon. Kaga.

Nagatsune. Yasui. 1670. Ichinomiya, Echizen. A great expert. Pupil of Yasui Takanaga. Kyoto.

Nagatsune. Kashiwaya. 1770. Chiuhachi. He marked his works Setsuzan or Ganshoshi. In recognition of his extraordinary ability he received the title of Yechizen no Daijo, and was generally known as Ichi no Miya. He has few rivals and probably no superiors. A favorite design on his early carvings was the tsukushi (a kind of horse-tail grass) with addition of frogs, snails, etc., and his skill in producing these natural objects was extraordinary. Subsequently he chiselled dragons, shishi, figures, etc., with equal facility and accuracy. His artistic spirit is compared by Japanese connoisseurs to the moon rising over mountains; it is at once so high and so pure. He died in 1786. Kyoto.

Nagayori. Azuma. 1760. Matajiro. Commonly called Yeizui. A pupil of Noriyori (Hamano) and a skilled expert. His art name was Tsutembo. Yedo.

Nagayoshi. Kashiwaya. 1790. Son of Nagatsune, and almost equal to his father in skill. Kyoto.

Nagayoshi. 1690. Chozayemon. Kaga.

Nagayoshi. Ichikawa. 1710. Kinai. Not to be confounded with the great Kinai. Kaga.

Nagayoshi. 1750. Kiujiro; son of Nagashige Kuroyemon. Kaga.

Nagayoshi. 1640. Kanyemon. Kaga.

Nagayoshi. Ishiguro. 1840. Called himself Jizan. A skilled expert.

Nakagawa. Yoshizane. Present day. A skilled metal-chiseller of Bizen.

Nakahara. Yukitoshi. 18th and 19th cent. Metal-worker of Choshiu.

Nakayama. Shoyeki. 16th and 17th cent. Common name Yojuro. Originally an armourer, he settled (1585) in Kyoto, and acquired a high reputation.

Nakazato. Norinaga. Present day. A skilled metal-chiseller of Tokyo, who now devotes himself largely to cameo-cutting in shell.

Namekawa. Sadakatsu. Present day. Kinzokushi. A pupil of Shomin. Remarkably skilled in chiselling figures in relief and incised on iron, silver, shibuichi, etc.

Nampo. Vide Konkwan. This mark was used by one of the nineteenth century Kikugawa artists also.

Nanjo. 1780. A pupil of Chokuzui. Yedo.

Nomura. Family name. Vide Sotoku and Masatoki.

Naoaki. Oda. 1830. An expert of Satsuma, highly skilled in tempering iron and chiselling designs à jour.

Naofusa. 1780. Tetsuya Bunjiro. A pupil of Tetsuya Gembei. Kyoto.

Naofusa. Hamano. 1800. Art name, Hokiusai. A skilled expert. Yedo.

Naokata. Okamoto. 1780. Chobei the adopted son of Tetsuya Gembei, whose name he afterwards took. Kyoto.

Naokatsu. Inagawa. 1720. Bunshiro. A pupil of Naomasa (Yanagawa) and a skilled expert. Yedo.

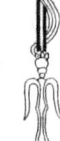

Naomasa. Yanagawa. 1690. Sanyemon. A pupil of Somin. A celebrated artist. His carvings of shishi (Dogs of Fo), horses, etc., are splendidly executed, and his nanako grounds are superb. His work is compared by Japanese connoisseurs to a waterfall among autumn foliage. In his later years he called himself Soyen. Yedo.

Naomasa. Ozaki. 1770. Magozayemon, or Kizayemon. Art name, Kichosai. A celebrated expert of Kyoto.

Naomichi. 1770. Shosuke. A pupil of Tetsuya Dembei. Kyoto.

Naomichi. Muneta. 1660. Matabe. Called also Dochoku. A celebrated expert. Worked chiefly in Osaka. His favourite subjects were human figures chiselled in the shishi-ai-bori and high-relief styles. Imitations abound, but are markedly inferior to the originals, which have been scarce ever since 1770.

Naomine. Muneta. 1660. Jisuke. Kyoto.

Naomitsu. Yanagawa. 1720. Rihei. A pupil of Naomasa, after whose death he took the name of Naomasa. A grand expert. Every stroke of the chisel is direct and strong. His work can scarcely be distinguished from that of Naomasa. Yedo.

Naonori. Konakamura. 1720. Kinchiro. A pupil of Naomasa. Yedo.

Naoshige. Kimura. 19th cent. Metal-worker of Yedo.

Naoshige. Okamoto. 1770. His common name was Tetsuya Gembei (Gembei, the worker in iron), but as he grew famous, men called him "Tetsugen," and sometimes "Tetsugendo." He was a pupil of Harukuni, who was known as Tetsuya Gembei. Many of his works are marked Shoraku, and some have Toshiyuki, his early name. He is held to be one of the greatest of Japanese artists.

His method of tempering iron and of producing patina is spoken of by Japanese writers of the eighteenth century as skilful beyond precedent. He worked also with consummate expertness in gold, silver, shakudo, and shibuichi. The *Soken Kisho* says that his work recalls the well-known couplet:
"How lovely is the cherry bloom touched by the morning sunbeams as they glance through the boughs of a pine tree!" He died in 1780, at a comparatively early age.

Naoshige. Muneta. 1680. Matashichi. Kyoto.

Naotaka. 1700. A pupil of Naomasa (Yanagawa). Yedo.

Naotmo. 1780. Ihei. A pupil of Tetsuya Gembei. Kyoto.

Naotoshi. Shimamura. 1700. A pupil of Naomasa (Yanagawa). Yedo.

Naotsugu. Shimizu. 1700. Jinyemon. A pupil of Naomasa (Yanagawa). Yedo.

Naoyasu. 19th cent. Metal-worker of Yedo. Art name, Kikodo.

Naoyori. Toyama. 1770. Denzo. An expert of note, who worked in Yedo, and afterwards Shinano and Yechizen. Called also Chokuzui (another pronunciation of Naoyori).

Naoyoshi. Sano. 1730. Rihachi. A pupil of Naonori; highly skilled. Carved for the Daimiyo Akimoto. Yedo.

Naoyuki. Yanagawa. 1700. Koheiji. A pupil of Naomasa. Some of his works are marked Yanagawa Naomasa. Yedo.

Narichika. 18th and 19th cent. Metal-worker of Yedo.

Narihisa. Hirata. 1650. Hikoshiro. Third representative of the Hirata family. Yedo.

Narikado. Hirata. 1700. Hikoshiro. Fifth representative of the Hirata family. Called also Henjo and Yeijo. Yedo.

Narikata. Umetada. 1740. Kajiyemon. Son of Naritsugu. Yedo.

Narikazu. Hirata. 1630. Hikoshiro. Second representative of the Hirata family. Yedo.

Narimasa. Hirata. 1840. Hikoshiro. Called also Riyozo and Genjo. Yedo.

Narisuki. Hirata. 1790. Hikoshiro. Called also Ichizo. Seventh of the Hirata experts. Yedo.

Naritsugu. Umetada. 1720. Kajiyemon. A Yedo expert of the highest skill. His carving is usually on a ground of shibuichi with profuse use of gold in the decorative design. Born in 1696, died 1735.

Nariwo. Shoami. 18th and 19th cent. Metal-worker of Matsuyama (Iyo).

Nariyuki. Hirata. 1740. Hikoshiro. Called also Kiuzo and Ichizo. The sixth representative of the Hirata family, and generally considered one of the best of the Hirata experts. Yedo.

Nariyuki. Hirata. 1880. Hikoshiro. Tokyo.

Natsuo. (d.1894.) A metal-chiseller of Tokyo, who is justly reckoned one of Japan's greatest experts.

Nihei. Muneta. 1560. The first maker of nanako grounds in the Muneta family. Kyoto.

Nishimura. Family name. Vide Mitsuyoshi.

Nizayemon. Muneta. 1540. Kyoto. There was a second Nizayemon (1580) in the same family.

Nobuaki. 1530. A pupil of Nobuiye. Celebrated for chiselling guards à jour, and for the beauty of his patina. Kuwana (Ise).

Nobuchika. Hirano. 1810. A pupil of Ontaiken. Mito.

Nobufusa. Miyochin. 1540. A great expert. Kai.

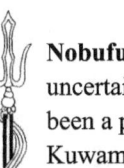

Nobufusa. Umetada. 1640. Date uncertain. Sei-no-jo. Supposed to have been a pupil of one of the early Kuwamura artists. A fine expert. Kaga.

Nobuhide. Sumitomo. 1750. Sennosuke. A pupil of Masanobu (Zenji). Yedo.

Nobuhiro. Miyochin. 1560. A great expert. Kamakura.

Nobuiye. Miyochin. 1520. One of the Nochino Sansaku (Three Later Masters) of the Miyochin family. Worked principally as an armourer, but also chiselled guarda. Joshiu.

Nobuiye. Fujiwara. 1670. A guard-maker of Aki. His work was in the pierced style, and he is celebrated for guards in the Mokko shapes with omodaka leaves chiselled à jour. His pieces are constantly confounded with those of Miyochin Nobuiye.

Nobuiye. 1700. A guard-maker of Kishiu. Not a good expert, but his work is often mistaken by ignorant collectors for that of Miyochin Nobuiye.

Nobukatsu. Kikuchi. 1730. Seijiro. Art name, Gitoken and Soriuken. A pupil of Naokatsu (Inagawa) and an expert of great skill. Yedo.

Nobumasa. Okada. 1690. Zenzayemon. A grandson of Meiju Umetada, who changed his family name Okada. Hagi.

Nobusada. 1530. A pupil of Nobuiye (Miyochin) and a skilled expert. Joshiu.

Nobushige. Okada. 1700. Hikozaye-mon. Hagi.

Nobutaka. Nara. 1730. Ihachi. Younger brother of the celebrated Masanaga, whose name he sometimes used. Yedo.

Nobutatsu. Hayashi. 19th cent. Skilled metal-worker of Yedo. Art name, Tokai.

Nobutsugu. Yoshioka. 1710. Choyemon. Called also Soin. A great expert. According to the *Soken Kisho* he was called Munenori. Yedo.

Nobutsune. Nakai. 1620. Bunyemon. The first of the Nakai family who worked in Hagi, Nagato province, and therefore the originator of the celebrated Choshiu guards (iron).

Nobuyasu. Saotomo. 1530. A pupil of Miyochin Nobuiye. Worked in Mito, where for many generations his family enjoyed the reputation of skilled armourers.

Nobuyoshi. Washizu. 19th cent. Skilled metal-worker of Yedo. Obtained the art title of Hogen.

Nobuyoshi. Miyochin. 1550. A celebrated metal-worker. Kamakura. Received the title of Hokkyo, and afterwards of Hogen.

Noriaki. Noda. 1815. Shirobei. Called himself Saiyoshin. A skilled carver and an able painter. Yedo.

Norikuni. Miyochin. 1560. A well known expert. Kozuke.

Norikyo. Goto. 1650. Shichibei. Kaga.

Norimasa. Nakagawa. 1750. A pupil of Noriyuki (Hamano). Yedo.

Norinao. Muneta. 1640. Matabei. Art name, Doki. A celebrated expert. He invented a special and particularly difficult style of nanako called daimiyo-nanako, in which the lines of nanako alternate with lines of polished ground. He is supposed to be the only expert who succeeded thoroughly in such work. Kyoto.

Norinobu. Hamano. 1790. Kimbei. A skilled artist. Used two of the art names employed by Shozui, viz., Otsuriuken and Miboku.

Norisada. Shoami. 1500. A Kyoto expert. His era is uncertain, and he is sometimes spoken of as the second founder of the Shoami family, though that position is more commonly assigned to Takatsune (q.v.).

Norishige. Miyochin. 1560. A skilled expert. Kozuke.

Noriyori. Hamano. 1750. Chiugoro. A pupil of Shozui, and a celebrated expert. A carving by him on the stone gate of Tentoku-ji cemetery of the Unshiu Daimiyo is one of the finest works of the kind in Japan. It represents the sixteen Disciples of Buddha, and was designed by the painter, Sasawa Hoin. Yedo.

Noriyuki. Hamano. 1740. A pupil of Shozui (Masayuki), but his style resembles that of Joi. An artist of the highest skill. Yedo.

Noriyuki. Nakamura. 1770. Gensuke. A pupil of the celebrated Nakahara Yukinori. Nagato.

Ogiya. Katsuhira. 19th cent. Metal-worker of Yedo. Art name, Seiriyo-ken.

Ohori. Masatoshi. 19th cent. (d.1897). A celebrated Uchimonoshi (metal-hammerer) of Tokyo.

Oishi. Akichika. 19th cent. Metal-worker of Yedo.

Okada. Setsuga. Present day. A highly skilled metal-chiseller of Tokyo. Has carved sword-furniture for the Emperor, and also diadems for the Emperor and Empress.

Okando. Vide Teruhiko (Murata).

Okazawa. Yeiseuke. 19th cent. Metal-worker of Choshiu.

Okimichi. Tokioka. 1680. Tosuke. Kyoto.

Okinari. Horiye. 1750. Yajiuro. Art name, Isshiken. A pupil of the celebrated Shozui. An artist of the first rank. Yedo.

Okiyoshi. 1770. Horiiye. Yaichiro. Son of Okinari, and a skilled artist. Served the feudal chief of Awa and worked in Yedo.

Okutsugu. Yoshioka. 1670. Hide-no- suke. Yedo.

Onishi. Hideo Naomura. 19th cent. Metal-worker of Yedo.

Ontaiken. Vide Motochika (Fujita).

Osaki. Toshiaki. 19th cent. Metal-worker of Yedo.

Otsuki. Family name. Vide Kworin.

Otsuriuken. Vide Masayori, Kaneyori, Norinobu, and Masanobu.

Rakurakusai. Vide Katsuyoshi.

Rakusuido. Vide Tsunenari.

Ranzan. Vide Tsuneyuki.

Reijō. Goto. 1650. Mitsuchika. Kyoto.

Rengetsutei. Vide Toshikage.

Renjō. Goto. 1650. Tenth of the great Goto Masters.

Rifudō. Vide Masayuki.

Rifudō. Vide Masayori and Masanobu.

Rinfudō. Vide Masaharu.

Rinjō. Goto. 1650. Mitsuzane. Kyoto.

Rinsendō. Vide Mitsumasa.

Risai. Motokawa. 1780. A Kyoto expert of the highest skill.

Risho. Iwamoto. 1800. Kinjiro. Called himself also Toshimasa. Yedo.

Risuke. Uyemura. 1720. A pupil of Munemine. Kyoto.

Ritsujo. Goto. 1600. Mitsuyori. Kyoto.

Ritsumei. Vide Koretsune.

Riujo. Goto. 1650. Mitsusada. Kyoto.

Riutnin. 19th cent. (d.1863). A splendid metal-chiseller of Yedo, who produced not only sword-furniture but all kinds of objects. Art name, Shoumsai.

Riurin-sai. Vide Hidetomo.

Riusen. Fujiki. 1660. Yojibei or Shigenori. Pupil of Goto Renjo and father of Masafusa (Fujiki). Kyoto.

Riushatei. Vide Takeaki.

Riu-un-sai. Vide Tomochika (Omori).

Riu-u-sai. Vide Teruhide (Omori).

Riyōkwan. Iwamoto. 1750. Yohachi. Teacher of the celebrated Konkwan, and himself a skilled expert. Yedo.

Riyonenshi. Yasuyobi. 19th cent. Metal-worker of Yedo.

Riyōyei. Iwamoto. 1770. Suzuki Kinyemon. Pupil of Iwamoto Konkwan. Remarkably good at carving fish designs. Yedo.

Riyōyen. Vide Masayuki.

Riyōyu. Vide Morikatsu and Morihiro.

Riyozō. Vide Narimasa.

Rizui. Vide Toshiyori.

Rokuyemon. Saito. 1800. A skilled inlayer of Sendai.

Saburoyemon. Yamanaka. 1630. Pupil of Goto Yekijo, and a grand artist. Kyoto.

Saburozayemon. Kurose. 1630. Pupil of Goto Seijo. Kyoto.

Saburozayemon. Inouye. 1650. Founded the house called Sammon-ji-ya, and developed an original style of carving called Oike-bori, from the name of the street (Oike-dori) in which he lived. Kyoto.

Sadachika. Nogi. 1790. Mohei. A pupil of Terusada (Yamamoto). Yedo.

Sadahide. 1840. Yasokichi. A pupil of Jikyokusai. Yedo.

Sadahiro. Shoami. 1560. Worked in Owari, following the style of Yamayoshibei.

Sadahisa. Morita. 1810. Sogoro. Called himself Tosuiken. A pupil of Chikuzanken, and a skilled expert. Mito.

Sadahisa. Takahashi. 1800. Masabei. Called himself Shosensai. A pupil of Chikuzanken and a skilled expert. Mito.

Sadakage. 1650. Shinyemon. Kaga.

Sadakatsu. Taneda. 1630. Kichinojo. A pupil of Goto Yenjo and a skilled expert. Kaga.

Sadakatsu. 19th cent. Metal-worker of Yedo.

Sadasuke. Inuma. 1800. A Mito expert, pupil of Chikuzanken.

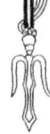

Sadatoki. 1630. Heihachi. A skilled expert who worked originally in Fushima, and moved to Kaga in the year 1625. He received a grant of three hundred koku of rice annually from the feudal chief of Kaga.

Sadatsugu. 1680. Kichirokuro. Kaga.

Sadatsugu. Yoshioka. 1780. Kichi-jiro. Yedo.

Sadatsugu. 1800. A pupil of Sadachika (Nogi). Yedo.

Sadayoshi. Fujita. 1840. Anshi. Called himself Kingenshi. Yedo.

Sadayoshi. 1770. A pupil of Nagatsune. A skilled expert. Yamashina (Yamashiro).

Sadayuki. 1840. Kinjiro. A pupil of Jikyokusai. Yedo.

Saihaku. Vide Masayoshi.

Saijiro. Goto. 1630. Kaga. (Vide Yoshisada.)

Saika-an. Vide Mitsuyuki. (Kikuoka.)

Saiyoshin. Vide Noriaki.

Sakuma. 1600. Date uncertain. Nothing is known of this expert, but some very fine specimens of iron guards bearing his signature are extant.

Sakuyemon. Chiyo. 1700. A pupil of Kuisuke of Tsuyama. Succeeded by his son of the same name.

Sakuyemon. Chiyo. 1700. There were two artists of this name, father and son. They worked at Tsuyama.

Sammonji-ya. Vide Saburozayemon and Kuhei.

Sano. Naotsune. 19th cent. Metal- worker of Yedo.

Sano. Takachika. Present day. A metal-chiseller of Tokyo.

Saotomo. Vide Nobuyasu.

Sasaki. Family name. Vide Shigekata, Tadatsura, etc.

Sato. Yoshi. 19th cent Metal-worker of Yedo.

Seibei. Shoami. 1760. Worked at Nihonmatsu in Aizu.

Seijiro. Goto. 1630. A great expert; but not well known. Kaga.

Seijo. Goto. 1630. Mitsunaga. Kyoto.

Seimin. Murata. 1820. Sozaburo. A celebrated chiseller, but chiefly remarkable for his skill in casting bronzes. Yedo.

Seiriyoken. Vide Ogiya Katsuhira.

Seiroku. Vide Masanaga (Nara) and Masachika (Nara).

Seiseisai. Vide Masatoki.

Seishichi. Shoami. 1840. A guard-maker of Osaka.

Seishinken. Vide Mototomo.

Seiunsai. Vide Motoshige (Mimura).

Seiunsai. Vide Taki Yeiji.

Seiunsha. Vide Toho.

Seizayemon. Goto. 1670. An artist of remarkable skill. Kaga.

Seki. Yoshinori. 19th cent. Metal-worker of Yedo.

Sekibun. Shoami. 1820. Shichiroyemon. Art name, Yurosai. Worked at Shonai in Dewa.

Sekiguchi. Ichiya. 19thcent. (d.1895). A skilled metal-chiseller of Tokyo. One of the last of the carvers of sword-furniture.

Sekijō. Goto. 1570. Mitsutsune. Son of Goto Takujo. Kyoto.

Sekijōken. Vide Motozumi (Yasuyama).

Senjo. Goto. 1620. Mitsukyo. Kyoto.

Sensai. Vide Atsuoki.

Senshichi. Nishiyama. 1640. A pupil of Goto Yenjo. Kyoto.

Senshisai. Vide Shoami.

Senyushi. Vide Yoshitsune.

Setsuju. 1780. A skilled expert of Mito, said to have been connected with the Miyochin family.

Setsuya. 19th cent. Art name of a Yedo metal-worker.

Setsuzan. Vide Nagatsune.

Shiatsu. Shinji. Present day. Metal-sculptor. Pupil of Unno Shomin.

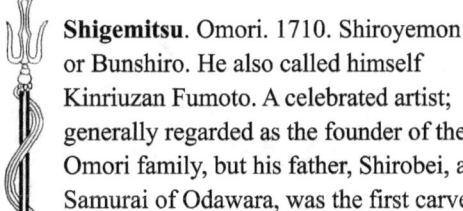

Shichibei. 1700. A renowned inlayer. His skill was so great that the name Zoshichi came to be applied to particularly fine damascening. Kyoto.

Shichirobei. Shoami. 1710. A pupil of Katsusaburo. Worked at Tsuyama in Mimasaka.

Shigeaki. 19th cent. Metal-worker of Yedo.

Shigechika. Machida. 1740. Kinzo. A pupil of Soyo, and a skilled expert. His father, also called Kinzo, worked in the same way but with less skill. Yedo.

Shigechika. Yokoya. 1720. Called also Machida. Kuizo.

Shigeharu. Nara, 1710. A pupil of the first Toshinaga. Common name, Jiubei.

Shigehiro. Yoshioka. 1580. Morotsugu. Called also Sotaku. He had the title at first of Buzan-no-suke and afterwards of Inaba-no-suke. Founded the Yoshioka family. Yedo. With regard to the title Inaba-no- suke, which is found on some of the works of the Yoshioka family and not on others, the explanation is that its use in such a manner was interdicted when a member of the noble family of Inaba happened to hold the office of Goroju. The Yoshioka family worked for the Yedo Court and had a yearly allowance of two hundred koku of rice and eighteen rations.

Shigekata. Sasaki. 1630. Common name not known. A Kyoto expert of some repute.

Shigekuni. Miyochin. 1560. A great expert of Kozuke.

Shigemichi. Shoami. 1760. A Kyoto expert, celebrated for chiselling guards with clam-shell decoration à jour.

Shigemitsu. Omori. 1710. Shiroyemon or Bunshiro. He also called himself Kinriuzan Fumoto. A celebrated artist; generally regarded as the founder of the Omori family, but his father, Shirobei, a Samurai of Odawara, was the first carver in that family. Yedo.

Shigemitsu. Nara. 1720. Yedo.

Shigemitsu. 18th cent. Metal-worker of Yedo. Pupil of Nara Yasuchika.

Shigemoto. Kubo. 1780. Commonly known as Tetsuya Kimbei. A pupil of the celebrated Tetsuya Dembei, and himself very famous. Many of his works are marked Takenori. Kyoto.

Shigemune. Shoami. 1840. An expert of Yedo.

Shigemune. Umetada. 1400. Known as Hiko no Shin. Said to be the nineteenth representative of the Umetada family, but probably identical with the first Shigeyoshi (vide). He received the name Umetada from the Emperor Shoko.

Shigenaga. 1680. Shinshichi. Successor of Tomotsugu Saburoyemon. Kaga.

Shigenaga. Yoshioka. 1640. Rizayemon. Afterwards called Sorin and Shigemoto. Yedo.

Shigenobu. 1780. Kitaro. A pupil of Tetsuya Dembei.

Shigenori. Miyochin. 1560. An expert of Kozuke.

Shigesada. Shoami. 1690. A pupil of Goto Tsujo. Worked at Akita in Dewa.

Shigesada. Yoshioka. 1840. The ninth representative of the Yoshioka family. Yedo.

Shigetaka. Hirata. 1680. Hikoshiro. Fourth representative of the Hirata family. Yedo.

Shigetsugu. Yoshioka. 1620. A member of the noble Fujiwara family. Had at first the title of Bun-gon-no- suke. Also called Soju. He became carver to the Court of the Yedo Shogun in the year 1600, and died in 1653. In the temple Zojo-ji, at Shiba (Tokyo), there is a stone carving by him representing the entry of Buddha into Nirvana. The inscription shows that it was carved in his 73d year.

Shigetsugu. Iwai. 1650. Moyemon. A pupil of Goto Renjo. Kyoto.

Shigetsugu. 1700. Kihashiro. Son of Shigenaga Shinshichi. Kaga.

Shigetsugu. Nara. 1720. A pupil of Toshinaga the second.

Shigetsune. 19th cent. Metal-worker of Choshiu.

Shigetsune. Shoami. 1720. Worked at Wakamatsu in Aizu.

Shigetsune. Shoami. 1650. An expert of Akita in Dewa.

Shigeyasu. Inouye. 1740. Bunjiro. A celebrated expert. Kyoto.

Shigeyoshi. Umetada. 1400. A celebrated sword-smith, who is said to have made guards for the Ashikaga Shogun, Yoshimitsu, the great art patron and dilettante of mediaeval Japan. Kyoto.

Shigeyoshi. Umetada. 1560. Hiko-jiro. He also used the name Miyoju for marking his pieces. An expert of very high order. He forged sword-blades which are held in the greatest esteem, and made guards and other mounts with equal skill. He was employed by Yoshioka, the last of the Ashikaga Shoguns, by Hideyoshi, the Taiko, and by Hidet-sugu. He worked from 1550 to 1600. Kyoto.

Shigeyoshi. Umetada. 1630. Hiko-jiro. He marked his pieces Meishin, or more commonly, lyetaka. He was counted a great sword-smith as well as a skilled carver, and received from the government the honorary title of Hokkyo.

He worked in Kyoto and Yedo, and it is supposed that the various provincial artists calling themselves by the family name of Umetada were either pupils of his or descended from his pupils.

Shigeyuki. Shoami. 1820. One of the Yedo branch of the Shoami family.

Shikō. Shoami. 1700. An expert of Kyoto who worked in the style of Sōden (Ed. Sōten).

Shimada. Family name. Vide Masafusa and Masanao.

Shinjō. Vide Mitsuyoshi (Goto).

Shinryo. Vide Koretsune.

Shinshichi. 1730. A skilled expert of Osaka, commonly known as Hori-mono-ya Shinshichi (Shinshichi, the carver). His favorite design was a fishing rod and river trout, which he chiselled beautifully.

Shintōken. Vide Mitsuyoshi.

Shijun. Vide Masayori. Shiratoshi. Iwamoto. 19th cent. Skilled metal-worker of Yedo. Used the marks Kwanri and Jounsai.

Shirobei. Muneta. 1650. Kyoto and Gifu (Mino).

Shisuido. Vide Kakuriyo. Shiuko. 19th cent. Metal-worker of Yedo.

Shōami. Vide Masanori.

Shōbei. Goto. 1570. A pupil of Goto Tokujo. Lived at various places, but chiefly Noto and Kyoto.

Shogoro. 1790. A pupil of Tashichi (Akao), and a skilled worker in the Akao style. Yedo.

Shōho. Iwamoto. 1830. Buto Gempachi or Masakatsu. An expert of considerable note. Many of his pieces are marked Konkwan-mon, i.e., pupil of Konkwan. Yedo.

Shōjō. Goto. 1610. Mitsumasa. Kyoto.

Shōjō. Goto. 1530. Younger brother of Goto Sojo. Celebrated as a maker of nanako grounds. Kyoto.

Shōjū. Tamagawa. 1760. Saburohei.
A pupil of Tsuju, and a great expert.
Yedo and Mito.

Shōkatei. Vide Katsutane.

Shōmin. 19th cent. A celebrated metal-worker of Tokyo, now living; art name, Senshisai.

Shōsensai. Vide Sadahisa (Takahashi).

Shotayu. Vide Masanao.

Shōyei. 1640. He called himself Johaku.
A pupil of Jochiku, and a skilled expert.
Yedo.

Shōyei. Vide Johaku.

Shōzayemon. Yoshioka. 1630.
Second son of Shigetsugu.
Carver to the Shogun's Court in Yedo.

Shōzayemon. Nomura. 1530.
A pupil of Goto Shojo. Kyoto.

Shizui. Vide Masayon.

Shuchin. Furukawa. 1820.
Son of Jochin and a skilled expert. Yedo.

Shuhōsai. Vide Masayori.

Shūjō. Goto. 1620. Mitsutoyo. Kyoto.

Shūjō. Goto. 1690. Mitsutaka. Kyoto.

Shumin. 19th cent. (d.1866).
A highly skilled metal-chiseller of Tokyo.

Shungetsu. Vide Haruaki.

Shunjō. Goto. 1640. Mitsunaga. Kyoto.

Shunshōdō. Vide Konkwan.

Shunzui. Vide Haruyori.

Shuraku. 19th cent. (d.1860).
A great metal-chiseller of Yedo: pupil of
Temmin and of Shugetsu. Many beautiful
specimens of his work are extant in
sword-furniture, pouch-clasps, and chains
(kuda-gus-ari), etc. He used the marks
Taido Shuraku, and Shuunsai Shuraku.

Shuzui. Vide Hideyori.

Sōchi. Yokoya. 1640. Tsugusada. Yedo.

Sōden. Kitagawa. (Ed. Sōten) 1649.
Originally called Hidenori. Celebrated as
a maker of iron sword-guards, elaborately
decorated with figure designs chiselled à
jour.

He used the mark Soheishi, and this
being commonly misread "mogarashi,"
the guards of Sōden's type are known as
mogara-shi-tsuba. They are exceptionally
large, and generally have the edge
curved. He belonged to the Shoami
family, according to some authorities,
and to the Kitagawa according to others.
Worked at Hikone, and originated the
Hikone style.

Sōheishi. Vide Sōden. (Ed. Sōten)

Sōhō. Vide Munemine.

Sōin. Yoshioka. His name is sometimes
pronounced Munenori. A great expert.
Yedo.

Sōin. Vide Nobutsugu.

Sōjo. Goto. 1520. The second of the great
Goto Masters. Kyoto.

Sōju. Vide Shigetsugu (Yoshioka)

Sōju. Vide Genchin.

Sōkan. Vide Toshimitsu (Nara).

Sōkei. Vide Munetsugu.

Sōken. Ozaki. 1630. Jiubei.
A pupil of Goto Teijo. Kyoto.

Sōken. Vide Muneaki.

Sokuseui. Goto. 1660. Kyto.

Sōkwan. Iwamoto. 1750. Kohachi. Yedo.
A great expert. (His name is also
pronounced Munehiro.)

Sōmin. Yokoya. 1760. Tomatsugu.
Grandson of the great Somin.
A skilled expert. Yedo.

Sōmin. Kiriusai. 1770. Representative of
the fourth generation of the Sōmin.

Sōmin. Yokoya. 1710. Tomotsune, or
Jihei. Art name, To-an. One of the most
celebrated experts of any era. Worked
from designs furnished by the painters
Tanyu and Hana-busa Itcho. Much of his
finest work was in the Kebori (hair-line
engraving) style, and he thus came to be
known as the originator of the Ye-fu-kebori (engraved pictures).

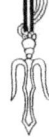

A Japanese connoisseur of the eighteenth century says that the impression produced by Sōmin's work is that of wooded hills reflected in the blue waters of a placid lake as the evening moon rises over their summit. True name, Tomotsune. Yedo. Many of his pieces are marked Tonan.

Sonjō. Another name for Goto Shojo.

Sonobe. Yoshiteru. 18th and 19th cent. Metal-worker of Yedo.

Sonobe. Yoshitsugu. 19th cent. Metal-worker of Yedo.

Sōri. Yokoya. 1710. A pupil of Sōmin. Yedo.

Sōrin. Vide Shigenaga.

Sōriusai. Vide Yoshinori.

Sōtei. Vide Toshimune (Nara). The name Sotei is sometimes pronounced Munesada.

Sōtetsu. Fujinaka. 1600. A pupil of Goto Yeijo. Kyoto.

Sōtoku. Nomura. 1580. Pupil of Goto Takujo. Founded the Nomura family. Kyoto.

Sōyei. Iwamoto. 1800. Heijiro. Yedo.

Sōyen. Vide Naomasa.

Sōyō. Yokoya. 1740. Tomosada. Art name, Kiriusai. Son of Somin, and almost as skilled as his father. Yedo.

Sōyō. Yokoya. 1630. Founder of the Yokoya family. Worked for the Court in Yedo. True name, Moritsugu. Yedo. A celebrated artist. Had a yearly allowance of two hundred bales of rice and twenty rations from the Yedo Court.

Sōyū. Vide Toshiharu (Nara).

Sōyū. Vide Teruaki (Yokiya).

Sugiyama. Toshiyoshi. 18th and 19th cent. Metal-worker of Mito.

Sukesaburo. Umemura. 1640. A pupil of Tomihisa (Kawamura), and a skilled expert. Kaga.

Sukeyori. 1800. Commonly called Jozui. A pupil of Tozui. Yedo.

Sumpei. Ichiju. Present day. Metal-sculptor. Pupil of Unno Shomin.

Sunagawa. Masayoshi. 19th cent. Metal-worker of Yedo. Art name, Shohakudo.

Suzuki. Gensuke. Present day. A skilled uchimomo-shi of Tokyo. Art names, Reiunsai and Suzugen. Seven generations of this family lived and worked in Yedo (Tokyo), the seventh, Suzuki Gensuke (q.v.), being the present representative. The first six manufactured chiefly metal pen-boxes for the girdle, (ya-tate), incense-boxes (kogo), etc. They used the mark Genshin.

Suzuki. Katsuyasu. 19th cent. Metal-worker of Yedo. Son of Ogiya Katsuhisa.

Tadahira. 1630. Saburohei. Went from Fushimi to Kaga.

Tadakyo. 1650. Shotaro; son of Tadahira Saburobei. Kaga.

Tadamichi. 1700. A Kyoto expert. Family unknown.

Tadashige. Ishikawa. 1820. Jiujiro. A pupil of Tadatsugu (Yoshioka). Yedo.

Tadasuke. Tsuji. 1770. Used the mark Teisuido. A highly skilled expert. Worked in Omi.

Tadatsugu. Yoshioka. 1800. Daijiro. Yedo. A great expert.

Tadatsugu. Shoami. 1670. A Kyoto expert.

Tadatsune. Wakabayashi. 1820. Hikoshiro. A pupil of Tadatsugu (Yoshioka). Yedo.

Tadatsura. Susaki. 1680. Saburohei. Osaka.

Tadayasu. 1750. A curio-dealer of Yedo. Ito Saburohei by name, had a quantity of fine sword-mounts carved with the inscription Tadaya-su, a combination of ideographs corresponding to his name. The work is in the style of Hamano Noriyuki.

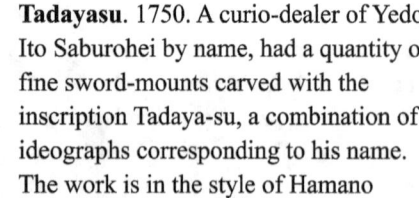

Tadayori. Hamano. 1790. Samurosuke. A skilled expert. Generally known as Tozui (another pronunciation of Tadayori). Yedo.

Tadayoshi. Nomura. 1740. Hanshichi. Yedo.

Tadayoshi. A pupil of Tsu Jimpo. Yedo. Tadayoshi. 1750. Common name unknown and date approximate. Specimens bearing his name are sometimes found. The ground is polished, and the design is an official cap (kammuri) and an umbrella chiselled in relief. The same name is found on guards evidently by a different hand.

Tadayoshi. Nomura. 1750. Commonly known as Tsuji Heihachi. A pupil of Tsu Jimpo and a skilled expert. Yedo.

Tadayoshi. Akao. 1840. A pupil of the Akao family, and a skilled guard-maker. Yedo.

Tadayuki. Asagawa. 1820. Miyagoro. A pupil of Tadatsugu (Yoshioka). Yedo.

Taguchi. Katsuo. Present day. Metal-sculptor. Pupil of Unno Shomin.

Taijō. Goto. 1660. Kyoto.

Taijō. Goto. 1660. Mitsuhisa.

Taizanken. Vide Yenju.

Takaaki. Ishiguro. 1850. Mankichi. Yedo.

Takafusa. Uyemura. 1740. Kuhei. A great expert. Kyoto.

Takahiro. Yasui. 1690. Heiyemon. His house was called Kashiwaya, and he marked his works Chiriuken. A skilled artist. Kyoto.

Takaiishi. Shigeyoshi. Present day. (b.1838). Originally a chiseller of sword-furniture, renowned for his skill in cutting kiri-mon (i.e., designs on the surface of sword blades), but now celebrated for the production of iron dragons, craw-fish, crabs, etc., with universal joints after the manner of Miyōchin Yoshihisa.

Many of his productions have been sold as genuine examples of Miyochin's work. His hawks, eagles, etc., chiselled in silver and inlaid with gold are among the finest specimens of metal work ever produced.

Takakiyo. Sakawa. 1800. Gensaburo. Called himself Joyeiken. A skilled artist. Mito.

Takakusai. Vide Yoshihisa.

Takamitsu. Shoami. 1620. Founder of the Aizu branch of the Shoami family. Marked his work "Matsumura Genshichiro." Worked at Wakamatsu.

Takanaga. Yasui. 1670. Torabei. A pupil of Yasui Yoshinaga. Used the mark Fuko. Kyoto.

Takasu. Yeiji. 19th cent. Skilled metal-worker of Yedo. Art name, Horiuken.

Takatsune. Shoami. 1480. Jirohachi. A Kyoto expert, who resumed the profession of ornamental metal-worker commenced by his ancestor Masanori (vide), and is consequently known as the second founder (Chiukokaizan) of the Shoami family.

Takeakira. Masabayashi. 1800. Date uncertain. Personal name, Zusho, and art name, Riushatei. A skilled expert of Kyoto. A man of noble family.

Takechika. Sano. 19th cent. A skilled metal-worker of Yedo. Used the marks Issai Hoshu Gendo-jin and Shuki Hozan Issai.

Takemitsu. 1760. Uhei. A pupil of Tetsuya Dembei. Kyoto.

Takenori. Vide Shigemoto (Kubo).

Takenori. Okamoto. 1780. Uhei. Kyoto.

Takenori. 19th cent. Yedo.

Takeshima. Family name. Vide Ichiju.

Takeshita. Shoju. Present day. Metal-sculptor. Pupil of Unno Shomin.

Takeyama. Mahiko. Present day. A metal-chiseller of Osaka.

Taki. Yeiji. 19th cent. Skilled metal-worker of Yedo. Art name, Sei-un-sai.

Takujō. Goto. 1570. The fifth of the great Goto Masters. Kyoto.

Tamagawa. Joyei. 19th cent. Metal-worker of Yedo.

Tanaka. Family name. Vide Ichiroyemon.

Taneda. Family name. Vide Sadakatsu.

Tankai. Vide Toshikage.

Tankasai. Vide Motoakira. (Suzuki.)

Tansai. Hirata. 1620. Founded the Hirata family of Awa. Nothing is known of his work and his date is uncertain.

Tanzendō. Vide Yoshitatsu.

Tashichi. Akao. 1780. Generally known as Akao Yoshitsugu, but not to be confounded with Akao Yoshitsugu Kohei. A skilled expert of Yedo, remarkable for his chiselling à jour, and his production of patina.

Tatsufusa. Nara. 1730. A pupil of Yasuchika. Yedo.

Tatsujō. Goto. 1650. Mitsufusa. Kyoto.

Tatsumasa. Nara. 1710. A pupil of Toshinaga. Yedo.

Tatsunari. Arakawa. 1790. Tatsuzo. Brother of Terutoki (Omori).

Tazayemon. Nomura. 1660. A pupil of Goto Renjo and a skilled artist. Kyoto.

Teijō. Goto. 1630. The ninth Goto Master.

Teikan. 19th cent. Metal-worker of Tokyo.

Teisuidō. Vide Tadasuke.

Temmin. 19th cent. (d.1845). A Yedo metal-chiseller of the highest skill. He was a pupil of the second Kikugawa and a contemporary of Riumin, with whom he often worked conjointly, the two putting their names on the same specimen. Temmin used the marks Okina Temmin (i.e., old man Temmin); Shojō-okina Temmin.

Tempo. Shoami. 1700. A Kyoto expert, celebrated for carving flowers and leaves tossed by the wind. His pieces are generally marked Yamashiro no Kuni Tempo.

Tenjō. Vide Mitsunori. Goto.

Tenkōdō. Vide Hidekuni.

Teruaki. Yokoya. 1730. Originally known as Ishikawa Kiuhachi and afterwards called himself Jiriuken and Yumin. A great carver, but he devoted much of his labour to copying the masterpieces of others. A Japanese connoisseur of the eighteenth century writes: "No one could equal him in ease and rapidity of working. If he were asked to make a carving of some particular object on a kozuka, he would at once take up his chisel, did he happen to be in the mood, and would not cease till he had produced several exquisite specimens, working, all the while, in the simplest, most unconcerned way." Yedo.

Teruaki. Yokoya. 1700. Iyemon. Subsequently called himself Soyu. A skilled expert, but his works are very rare. Yedo.

Teruhide. Omori. 1760. Kisoji. Called himself Ittosai and Riu-u-sai. A pupil of Terumasa (Omori). A splendid expert. The Omori style (carving in high relief on grounds inlaid with gold in the aventurine pattern) became widely popular in his hands. The *Soken Kisho* says of him: "His chisel marks have a force that would rend a rock. His fuka-bori (deeply incised) waves, etc., on a ground of shibuichi are magnificent, and nothing can exceed the exquisite beauty of his high relief peonies on nashiji (aventurine ground). He seems to have based his method of carving flowers on Somin's celebrated ichi-rin-botan

(single-blossom peony). His martial figures are grand." Yedo. (Said to have been the first to carve wave diaper in high relief.)

Teruhiko. Murata. 1800. Bennosuke. Called himself Okando. Pupil of Teruhide (Omori). Yedo.

Teruhisa. Kuwamura. 1780. Kiuhei. Pupil of Terumasa (Omori). Yedo.

Teruiye. Omori. 1780. Denro. Pupil of Terumasa (Omori). Yedo.

Terukazu. Omori. 1760. Jisuke. Called himself also Kanshikan. Yedo.

Terukuni. Omori. 1810. Yagohei or Yajiuro. A great chiseller of nanako. Yedo.

Terumasa. Omori. 1730. A skilled expert, generally regarded as the originator of the Omori style. A pupil of Naomasa (Yanagawa). Art name, Yoichi Kambun. Yedo.

Terumitsu. Omori. 1820. Kisoji or Manzo. Called himself Chosendo and Kijusai. A great expert. Yedo.

Terumoto. Omori. 1810. Tatsuzo. Yedo.

Terunaga. Omori. 1790. Shirobei or Shigetsugu. Yedo.

Terusada. Yamamoto. 1780. Kambei. A pupil of Terumasa (Omori) and a skilled expert. Yedo.

Terushige. Yokoya. 1750. Minosuke. Sometimes marked his works Nobusada. Yedo.

Terutake. Suguira. 1780. Dembei. Pupil of Terumasa (Omori). Yedo.

Terutoki. Tokuno. 1780. Genjiro. Called himself also Ichimudo. A pupil of Terumasa (Omori) and a highly skilled expert. Yedo.

Terutoki. Omori. 1750. A pupil of Terumasa (Omori). Yedo.

Terutsugu. Yokoya. 1780. Yedo.

Terutsugu. Yoshioka. 1680. Rizayemon. Called also Hidesaburo, and had the title of Inaba-no suke. Yedo.

Terutsumu. Yoshioka. 19th cent. Metal-worker of Yedo.

Teruuji. Omori. 1800. Yojiuro or Teruchika. Yedo.

Teruyoshi. Mizuno. 1660. Genji. Kaga.

Tessai. Vide Yoshitatsu.

Tetsuya. Gembei. Vide Naoshige.

Tetsuya. Gembei. Vide Naoshige.

Tetsuya. Kimbei. Vide Shigemoto (Kubo).

Tetsuya. Dembei Vide Kuniharu and Harukuni.

Tōan. Vide Somin.

Tōdaya. Vide Mitsusada.

Tōgindo. Vide Yoshiteru.

Tōgokushi. Vide Masatsune and Koretsune.

Togu. Vide Motozumi (Oyama).

Tōhōken. Vide Motohisa (Yoshikawa).

Tōji. Tamagawa. 1820. Ginjiro or Ginsaburo. His works are often marked Katsuzumi. A skilled artist. Yedo.

Tōjū. Vide Hiromasa.

Tōkai. Vide Nobutatsu.

Tokakusai. Vide Yoshihisa.

Tokiakira. 1850. Art name, Issai. A Kyoto expert of great skill.

Tokihide. Kato. 1680. Jisuke. Kyoto.

Tokisada. 1630. Heihachi. A great expert. He received three hundred koku of rice annually from the feudal chief of Kaga for whom he worked.

Tokasai. Vide Hiramitsu. Tokuoki. 19th cent. Metal-worker of Yedo.

Tōmei. Present day. A skilled metal-chiseller of Osaka.

Tomejiro. Wakabayashi. 1790. Son of Masanao (Nomura). Yedo.

Tomihisa. Makita. 1760. Yayokichi, called also Hoju. Yedo.

Tomihisa. Kuwamura, 1630. Koshiro. A skilled expert of Kaga. The son of Moriyoshi.

Tominsai. Vide Yoshitsune.

Tomishige. Shoami. 1580.
Date uncertain. Worked in Owari.

Tomisuke. Uyemura. 1750. Sahei.
A pupil of Uyemura Takafusa. Kyoto.

Tomoakira. 1820. Date uncertain.
An expert of Bizen, skilled in the
Sumi-zogan process.

Tomobumi. 19th cent.
Skilled metal-worker of Yedo.
Art name, Yushinto.

Tomochika. Omori. 1820. Denzaburo.
Called himself Riu-un-sai.
A skilled expert. Yedo.

Tomoharu. Okamoto. 1590. Sojiro.
Hagi. Founded the Okamoto family
of Hagi.

Tomohiro. Takenouchi. 1810.
Kumayemon. Called himself
Ichigyokudo. Pupil of Hidetomo
(Omori). Yedo.

Tomokata. Okamoto. 1750. Kuma-no-jo.
Hagi.

Tomokiyo. Uyemura. 1700.
Hikozayemon. A skilled expert. Kaga.

Tomomasa. Hasegawa. 1810.
Yasunosuke. A pupil of Hidetomo
(Omori). Yedo.

Tomomasa. Daishinto. 1810. Tokichi.
A Samurai who became a pupil of
Hidetomo (Omori) and developed much
skill. Yedo.

Tomomichi. 1820. Vide Yoshiaki
(Tanaka). Tomomichi. 18th and 19th
cent. Metal-worker of Choshiu.

Tomomitsu. Onishi. 1810. Sadasuke.
A pupil of Hidetomo (Omori). Yedo.

Tomomitsu. Okamoto. 1630. Sayemon.
Hagi.

Tomonao. Yanagawa. 19th cent. Metal-
worker of Yedo. Art name, Kosetsuken.

Tomonobu. Nakai. 1700. Hikozayemon.
Hagi.

Tomonori. Hirose. 1810. Yoshiguro.
Pupil of Hidetomo (Omori). Yedo.

Tomosada. Vide Soyo (the 2d).

Tomoshige. 1630. Sukekuro.
Pupil of Tsuji Yamashiro no Kami.1640.

Tomotake. Yokoya. 1750. Yedo.

Tomotoshi. Okamoto. 1730. Kohei.
Hagi.

Tomotsugu. Vide Somin (the 2d).

Tomotsugu. Okamoto. 1690.
Tozayemon. An amateur who became
very famous. Hagi.

Tomotsugu. 1650. Saburoyemon.
Son of Tomoshige Sukekuro. Kaga.

Tomotsugu. Tsuji. 1700. Saburoyemon.
A skilled expert of Kaga.

Tomotsune. Omori. 1830. Keijiro. Yedo.
Some of his works are signed Hirano
Tomotsune.

Tomotsune. Nakai. 1680. Zensuke.
The most celebrated of the Choshiu
guard-makers of the Nakai family. His
iron guards chiselled in high relief in full
sculpture and à jour are of the highest
grade, and were selected by the feudal
chief of Choshiu for presentation to the
Tokugawa Government. Hagi.

Tomotsune. Nakai. 1640. Sahei. Hagi.
Not to be confounded with his celebrated
grandson of the same name.

Tomotsune. Vide Somin.

Tomoyoshi. Okamoto. 1670. Kohei.
Hagi.

Tomoyoshi. Okamoto. 1720.
Jinzayemon. Son of Tomotsugu. Hagi.

Tomoyoshi. Hitotsuyanagi. 1780.
There were two of this name, father
(1750) and son. They worked at Mito.

Tomoyoshi. Hirano. 1730. Izayemon,
Riyosuke. A master among the Mito
artists. Pupil of Yasuhira and employed
by the feudal chief of Mito.

Tomoyoshi. 1820. Vide Yoshiaki.

Tomoyoshi. Kikugawa. 19th cent.
Skilled metal-worker of Yedo. Art name,
Ichiriusai.

Tomoyuki. Nakai. 1700. Zembei. Hagi.

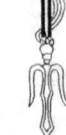

Tomoyuki. Nakai. 1660. Zensuke.
First of the Nakai family to carve figures, birds, animals, etc., and therefore the originator of the elaborately chiselled iron guards of Choshiu. Hagi.

Toriusai. Okano. 1850. Kijiro.
A Yedo expert of the highest skill. One of the greatest sculptors of sword-furniture in the nineteenth century. In 1846 he received the art rank of Hogen. Called also Kijiro.

Toshichi. 1720. A pupil of Masuya Kihei. Kyoto.

Toshiharu. Nara. 1680.
Employed by the Yedo Court. Famous for carving landscapes. Officially known as Echizen, and called Soyu in his old age. One of the three celebrated masters of the Nara family, who are commonly spoken of as "three pictures en suite " (san-buku-tsui), namely, Toshiharu, Toshihisa, and Yasuchika.

Toshihisa. Nara. 1760.
Son of the celebrated Toshihisa. Yedo.

Toshihisa. Nara. 1720. Tahei.
An artist of the highest fame. He is included with Toshiharu and Yasuchika in the group of the three Nara. Masters, known as the "three pictures en suite" (san-buku-tsui) . The *Soken Kisho* says of him : "His style was not that of either the Yokoya family or his own family. He carved plants, flowers, birds, etc., with the utmost delicacy, and is universally credited with having struck out a style of his own. The Nara school has found many imitators, but there is about Toshihisa's work an individuality that defies imitation. Nevertheless we find specimens carefully chiselled and marked Toshihisa. They cannot be compared to the genuine work any more than glass can be compared to diamonds." Yedo.

Toshikage. 19th cent.
Skilled metal-worker of Awaji. Art name, Tankai and Rengetsutei.

Toshikatsu. Nara. 1740. Called Chikugo in his old age. Yedo.

Toshimitsu. Watanabe. 19th cent.
Metal-worker of Yedo. Pupil of Toriusai.

Toshimitsu. 19th cent. Metal-worker of Yedo. Not to be confounded with Nara Toshimitsu.

Toshimitsu. Nara. 1720.
Shichirozayemon. Subsequently called Sokan. An expert of considerable fame. Yedo.

Toshimitsu. Vide Hisamitsu (Watanabe).

Toshimune. 19th cent. Metal-worker of Yedo.

Toshimune. Nara. 1630.
Son of Toshiteru. The first of the Nara experts to obtain distinction, and therefore often called the founder of the family. Called Sotei in his old age. Yedo.

Toshinaga. Nara. 1710.
A pupil of the first Toshinaga. Yedo.

Toshinaga. Nara. 1700. Shichizayemon.
An artist of considerable skill. Called Chizan in his old age. Yedo.

Toshinaga. 1700. An artist whose family and date are uncertain. His name is found on finely chiselled pieces, having a decoration of a cat-fish (numazu) and water-grasses in relief.

Toshinaga. Fujita. 1840.
An expert of Aizu, who worked in very elaborate style, but showed the inartistic features of the Aizu and Mino style.

Toshinao. Nara. 1750. Yedo.

Toshinobu. 19th cent. Metal-worker of Yedo. Art name, Unsuiken.

Toshioki. Kaneko. 1650.
Carver to the feudal chief of Kishiu.

Toshisada. 1720. Family, etc. unknown.
A guard-maker of Sado; highly skilled whether in chiselling à jour or in relief, and in tempering iron.

Toshishige. Nara. 1720.
A pupil of the second Toshinaga, Yedo.

Toshitayo. 19th cent.
Metal-worker of Yedo.

Toshiteru. Nara. 1620. Founder of the
Nara family of metal-workers.
Moved to Yedo in 1621. Yedo.

Toshitsugu. 19th cent.
Metal-worker of Yedo.

Toshitsune. Nara. 1770. Yedo.

Toshiyoshi. 19th cent.
Metal-worker of Yedo.

Toshiyoshi. Hamano. 19th cent.
Metal-worker of Yedo.

Toshiyori. Hamano. 1790. Nanjo.
Commonly called Rizui. Yedo.

Toshiyuki. 1750.
A pupil of Noriyuki (Hamano).

Tosuiken. Vide Sadahisa (Morita).

Tou. Vide Yasuchika (Nara).

Tōun. Vide Tamagawa Yoshihisa.

Tōunsai. Vide Masachika (Tsuji).

Tōunsai. Vide Hisatsugu.

Toyoda. Koko. Present day.
A skilled metal-chiseller of Tokyo; the
inventor of the process called kiri-bame-
zogan (vide text).

Toyokawa. Mitsunaga. Present day.
A metal-chiseller of Tokyo scarcely less
skilled than Shomin; son of Koriusai
(q.v.). He has made some magnificent
specimens, in which every kind of metal
work is employed.

Toyomasa. 18th and 19th cent.
Metal-worker of Choshiu.

Toyomitsu. Goto. 1720. Matsusaburo.
Kaga.

Toyosai. Vide Kanetomo.

Toyotaka. 19th cent.
Metal-worker of Choshiu.

Toyotomi. Minota. 1830. Yuho.
Pupil of Terumitsu (Omori). Yedo.

Toyoyori. Hamano. 1770. Hikogoro.
Generally known as Hozui (another
pronunciation of Toyoyori).
Art name, Tsugensai. Yedo.

Tōzui. Vide Tadayori.

Tsu-Jimpo. Vide Jimpo.

Tsuchiya. Family name. Vide Kinshichi.

Tsugensai. Vide Toyoyori.

Tsugusada. Vide Sochi.

Tsuji. 1630. Yamashiro-no-Kami.
Went from Fushimi to Kaga in the
year 1625.

Tsuji. 1700. Vide Tadayoshi.

Tsūjō. Goto. 1690. Eleventh of the great
Goto Masters. Kyoto.

Tsūjū. Vide Mitsuhisa.

Tsukuda. Shukiyo. Present day.
A skilled metal-sculptor, celebrated also
for combining metals so as to produce
fine effects of colour harmonies. He has
produced some magnificent iron tablets
with designs in high relief.

Tsunagawa. 19th cent.
Metal-worker of Yedo.

Tsunayoshi. Shoami. 1780.
Worked at Wakamatsu in Aizu.

Teunehisa. Kajima. 1810. Yeijiro.
A pupil of Kiyohisa (Tanaka). Yedo.

Tsunekatsu. Kikuchi. 1730.
A pupil of Naokatsu (Inagawa).
Celebrated for skill in chiselling in relief
and in the Kibori style. One of the great
artists of the Yanagawa school. Yedo.

Tsunekazu. Nara. 1720. Kiraku.
A pupil of Yasuchika. Yedo.

Tsunemitsu. Kikuchi. 1740. Iyemon.
A pupil of Tsunekatsu. Highly skilled in
Kibori chiselling, but his work lacks
strength.

Tsunenaga. 19th cent.
Metal-worker of Yedo.

Tsunenao. 1770. Kiubei.
A pupil of Nagatsune. Kyoto.

Tsunenari. Tsuji. 1760. Used the mark, Rakusuido. A great carver in the style of Rinsendo. He died young (Omi province).

Tsunenori. Nakai. 1600. Shinzayemon. Suwo.

Tsunesada. 1740. Yedo.

Tsuneshige. Nara. 1730. A great expert, celebrated for combining high and low relief. Used at first the mark Sekiguchi Ryoka, and afterwards that of Kawamura Ichiyemon. Yedo.

Tsunetsugu. Yoshioka. 1770. Rizayemon. Called also Hidesaburo, and had the title of Inaba-no-suke. Yedo.

Tsuneyuki. 19th cent. Metal-worker of Yedo. Art name, Jiriuken and Ranzan.

Tsuneyuki. 19th cent. Metal-worker of Yedo. Art name, Jiriyusai.

Uhei. Vide Jokwo.

Ujiharu. Wakabayashi. 1720. Uhei. A skilled artist. Originally of the Katsugi family, he changed his name to Wakabayashi, and became carver to the feudal chief of Toyama in Yetchiu.

Ujihira. Katsugi. 1770. Hachirobei. Kaga.

Ujihiro. Katsugi. 1720. Kichirobei. Celebrated for his nanako work. Kaga.

Ujiiye. Katsugi. 1630. Gondayu. Moved from Fushimi to Kaga in the year 1625. A pupil of Goto Kenjo and a skilled expert. He received an annual allowance of fifteen rations from the feudal chief of Kaga.

Ujiiye. Katsugi. 1650. Ichibei, son of Ujiiye Gondayu. Kaga.

Ujiiye. Kaneko. 1670. Ichibei, son of Ujiiye Katsugi, but subsequently changed his family name to Kaneko. A famous carver. Kaga.

Ujiiye. Katsugi. 1670. Ichiroyemon, younger brother of Ujiiye Ichibei. An artist of high repute. Kaga.

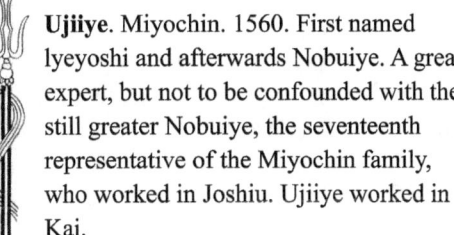

Ujiiye. Miyochin. 1560. First named Iyeyoshi and afterwards Nobuiye. A great expert, but not to be confounded with the still greater Nobuiye, the seventeenth representative of the Miyochin family, who worked in Joshiu. Ujiiye worked in Kai.

Ujikata. Katsugi. 1710. Kakunojo. Kaga.

Ujikiyo. Katsugi. 1690. KakubeL Kaga.

Ujimune. Katsugi. 1730. Saburo. Kaga.

Ujinaga. Katsugi. 1630. Kihei. Pupil of Ujiiye Gondayu. Kaga.

Ujinaga. Katsugi. 1650. Kihei, son of Ujinaga Kihei. Kaga.

Ujinao. Hirata. 1650. Ichizayemon. A pupil of the Shoami experts of Kyoto. A maker of iron guards inlaid with gold. Awa province.

Ujinari. 1670. Jihei. A pupil of Ujiiye Ichiroyemon. Kaga.

Ujinobu. Katsugi. 1670. Buhei; son of Ujiiye Ichibei. Kaga.

Ujinobu. 1670. A pupil of Ujiiye Ichiroyemon. Kaga.

Ujitada. 1670. A pupil of Ujiiye Ichiroyemon. Kaga.

Ujiteru. Wakabayashi. 1790. Kichirobei. Originally of the Katsugi family, he afterwards changed his name to Wakabayashi. Kaga.

Ujitsugu. Katsugi. 1670. Rokuro. Kaga.

Ujitsugu. Katsugi. 1790. Yenshichi. Kaga.

Ujiyasu. Hirata. 1680. Yohachiro. A maker of iron guards inlaid with gold. Awa province.

Ujiyasu. Katsugi. 1730. Kichirobei. Kaga.

Ujiyasu. Katsugi. 1750. Kichirobei. Kaga. (Second of the same name.)

Ujiyasu. Katsugi. 1760. Kichirobei. Kaga. (Third of the same name.)

Ujiyasu. Katsugi. 1780. Gonkichi. Kaga. (A pupil of Goto Yenjo.)

Ujiyoshi. Katsugi. 1750. Gonnojo. Kaga.

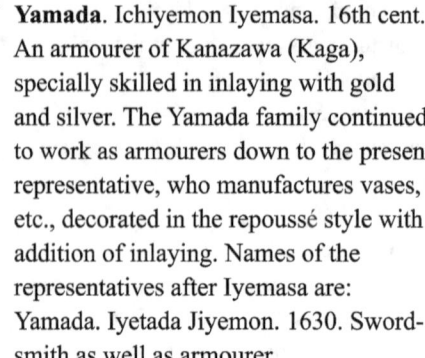

Ujiyoshi. Katsugi 1690. Ichinojo; son of Ujiiye Ichiroyemon. A celebrated artist, who combined delicate chiselling with rich inlaying. Kaga.

Ujiyoshi. Katsugi. 1790. Jihei. Kaga.

Unjō. Goto. 1680. Called also Mitsuyuki. Kyoto.

Unno. Nenokichi. A highly skilled metal-chiseller of the present day.

Unno. Shomin. Present day. One of the greatest workers in metal that Japan has produced. Originally a chiseller of sword-furniture. Has made many objects for the Imperial Court, and is famous for combining repousse and chiselling in iron, as well as for sculpture in the round, and for incised chiselling in the katakiri style.

Unno. Shoshiu. Present day. Metal-sculptor. Pupil of the Unno Shomin.

Unsui. Katsura. 1720. Nagatoshi. A pupil of Fusayoshi (Yokoya), and an artist of the first rank. Yedo.

Unsuiken. Vide Toshinobu.

Unteidō. Vide Hiranori.

Watanabe. Sukekuro. Vide Yasuyuki.

Watanabe. Hisamitsu. 19th cent. Metal-worker of Yedo.

Watanabe. Jizan. 19th cent. Metal-worker of Yedo.

Yagami. 18th and 19th cent. Metal-worker of Yedo.

Yahei. Kishimoto. 1780. A pupil of Goto Shichiroyemon, and a skilled artist of Kyoto.

Yamada. Gorobei. Muneyoshi. Present day. Son of Yamada Gorobei Munemitsu.

Yamada. Gorobei. Munemitsu. Present day. A metal-sculptor of Kaga, celebrated for his skill in repoussé work. He is the tenth in descent from Yamada Ichiyemon Iyemasa, who, as well as his descendants up to the time of the father of the present representative of the family, forged armour and iron stirrups inlaid with gold.

Yamada. Ichiyemon Iyemasa. 16th cent. An armourer of Kanazawa (Kaga), specially skilled in inlaying with gold and silver. The Yamada family continued to work as armourers down to the present representative, who manufactures vases, etc., decorated in the repoussé style with addition of inlaying. Names of the representatives after Iyemasa are:

Yamada. Iyetada Jiyemon. 1630. Sword-smith as well as armourer.

Yamada. Iyesada Gorobei. 1655.

Yamada. Iyetsugu Ichiyemon. 1685.

Yamada. Iyenaga Jinyemon. 1720.

Yamada. Nagakatsu Gorobei. 1760.

Yamada. Nagamoto Sanyemon. 1810.

Yamada. Nagayo Gorobei. 1840.

Yamada. Iyemitsu Gorobei. 1860.

Yamagata. A name given to the mark, meaning "mountain shape." The maker of the specimens thus marked has never been identified. They are generally decorated with herons, moorland views, spools of yam, etc., in relief on a polished ground, picked out with gold (not plating but solid gold). The maker cannot have lived at a later date than the middle of the eighteenth century.

Yamagawa. Koji. 19th cent. (d.1897). A skilled metal-chiseller of Takaoka.

Yamashiro-no-kami. Tsuji. 1630. Originally an artist of Fushimi, he moved to Kaga and received an allowance of one hundred and fifty koku of rice yearly from the feudal chief of that province.

Yamayoshi. Shoami. 1540. One of the old experts, contemporary with Nobuiye (Miyochin). He made guards with the design pierced à jour, but did not polish the iron. Worked in Owari.

Yamayoshi-bei. Shoami. 1570. Son of the first Yamayoshi. Worked in his father's style, but polished the iron carefully, and gave a recurved rim to his guards. Worked in Owari.

Yamazaki. Family name. Vide Ichiga.
Yanagawa. Family name. Vide Naomasa.
Yasayobi. Vide Riyonenshi.
Yasuchika. Tsuchiya (sometimes spoken of as Nara). 1730. Yagohachi.
A great artist, one of the "Three Nara Masters" (vide Toshihisa). His work resembles that of Toshihisa, but is bolder in style, and has a markedly subjective character. He had been called the Kworin (vide pictorial art) of glyptic artists. Imitations of his work have been numerous ever since the middle of the eighteenth century, but the essential features of his style are inimitable. Some of his pieces are marked Tou. Yedo.
Yasufusa. Hirata. 1700. Ichizayemon.
A maker of iron guards inlaid with gold. Awa province.
Yasuhira. Shinozaki. 1650. Shoyemon.
One of the most celebrated of the Mito experts. The Mito carving is more elaborate than artistic, but the technique is often admirable. Mito.
Yasuhisa. Shingaku. 1770. Tomo-no-jo. Artistic name, Keirinsai. Sendai.
Yasukawa. Sanyemon. 19th cent, (d.1887). A skilled metal-chiseller of Takaoka.
Yasunobu. Nara. 1730. Son of Yasuchika. Called at first Yasunobu. An artist scarcely inferior to his father, To-o. The representatives of the Yasuchika family worked generation after generation in Yedo, up to the sixth generation in 1850.
Yasunobu. Noda. 1600. Chiuzayemon. A skilled expert of Kyoto.
Yasushige. Fuse. 1630. Shozaburo. A pupil of Goto Sakujo. Kyoto.
Yasutomi. Shibayo. 1730. Ihei.
A pupil of Yokoya Teruaki. One of the earliest of the Sendai experts.
Yasuyemon. Komori. 1700.
A pupil of Goto Kambei. Kyoto.

Yasuyori. Hamano. 1770. Yenjuro.
At first called Naoyuki, and generally known as Hozui (another pronunciation of Yasuyori). Yedo.
Yasuyuki. Tsuji. 1750. An artist of note.
Had various names Masayuki, Watanabe, Sukekuro, and Hikokoro. Yedo.
Yeiji. Nayemura. 1820. A Kyoto expert, skilled in carving dragons among waves.
Yeijō. Vide Narikado (Hirata).
Yeijō. Goto. 1600. Sixth of the great Goto Masters. Kyoto.
Yeiju. Takase. 1780. Izayemon.
Pupil of Sekijoken.
Yeisendo. Vide Yoshinori.
Yeishu. Iwamoto. 1780. Yasuchika Shinsuke. Pupil of Iwamoto Konkwan. Celebrated for skill in Katakiri chiselling. Worked first in Yedo and afterwards in Mito.
Yeizui. Vide Fusayori.
Yekijō. Goto. 1630. Mitsuharu. Kyoto.
Yenjō. Goto. 1630. Mitsuhide, and commonly known as Kambei. Kyoto.
Yenjō. Goto. 1760. The thirteenth Goto Master.
Yetsujo. Goto. 1660. Mitsukuni. Kyoto.
Yohei. Umemura. 1710. Commonly called Masuya Yohei.
A pupil of Soho. Kyoto.
Yokoya. Family name. Vide Teruaki.
Yoritoshi. Nomura. Pupil of Hiyobu Hogen.
Yoritsune. 1580. Nothing is known about this artist, but an inscription on his work shows that he lived in the time of the celebrated master of tea ceremonial, Sen no Rikiu.
Yoshiaki. Tanaka. 1720. Gozayemon.
A pupil of Goto Rihei. A skilled expert. Yedo.
Yoshiaki. 1810. An expert of some note. Studied in Mito and settled in Yedo. Commonly called Unno Yoshiaki.

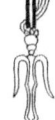

Yoshiaki. Ishiguro. 1850. Kichigoro. Yedo.

Yoshichika. Tsuchiya. 18th and 19th cent. Metal-worker of Kaga.

Yoshida. Family name. Vide Bunsui.

Yoshiharu. Kaneko. 1550. Kichi-no-jo. A man of noble origin, who studied carving under Goto Kwojo, and attained such skill that he adopted the work as a profession, and founded the Kaneko family of artists. Kyoto.

Yoshiharu. 1840. Sentaro. Yedo.

Yoshihide. Mikami. 1840. Wajiuro. Called Kosanya. Yedo.

Yoshihiro. Kuwamura. 1620. Yosabei. A skilled expert with a peculiarly soft style. Adopted son of Koko. Kaga.

Yoshihiro. Noda. 1730. Uhachi. A pupil of Yasuchika (Nara). Celebrated for carving groups of various kinds of fish. His work is tender yet strong. Yedo.

Yoshihiro. Iwamoto. 1750. Chiuyemon; afterwards Yohachi. Called also Kikwan. Father of the celebrated Konkwan (Iwamoto). He is sometimes spoken of as belonging to the Shoami family. Kyoto.

Yoshihisa. Umetada. 1700. The thirty-first descendant of Tachibana no Munechika. On his work is found the inscription Umetada Tachibana no Nanigashi, or "A certain member of the Tachibana family." A Kyoto expert.

Yoshihisa. 1810. Onominokichi. Art name, Tokakusai. A pupil of Kyohisa (Tanaka). Aizu.

Yoshihisa. Tamagawa. 1770. Saburoshiro. A skilled expert. Employed by the Daimiyo of Mito and afterwards worked in Yedo. Art name, Kiukiuken.

Yoshihisa. Tamagawa. 1790. Tashichi. Called himself Joyeikan. A nephew of Yoshihisa Saburoshiro. Celebrated for his skill in carving dragons. Yedo.

Yoshihisa. Shoami. 1750. Heisuke. Worked first at Tsuyama in Minosaka, and afterwards in Kyoto.

Yoshikawa. 19th cent. Metal-worker of Yedo.

Yoshikatsu. Inagawa. 1740. Carved in the style of Naomasa (Yanagawa) and attained a high reputation. Yedo.

Yoshikatsu. 1840. Yeijiro. A pupil of Jikosai. Yedo.

Yoshikatsu. Okamoto. 1740. Tozayemon. A skilled artist. His work was presented by the feudal chief of Choshiu to the Yedo Court. Hagi.

Yoshikazu. Shoami. 1620. An expert of the Iyo branch of the Shoami family. Matsuyama.

Yoshikuni. Yoshishige. 1660. Magoyemon. Kaga.

Yoshikuni. Yoshishige. 1710. Choyemon. Kaga.

Yoshikyo. Goto. 1630. Yoshishige. Employed at the Mint (Kobanza). Kyoto.

Yoshimitsu. Kaneko. 1660. An expert of Kii, sixth descendant of Yoshiharu Kichi-no-jo. Art name, Jogen. A skilled artist.

Yoshimitsu. Aoyagi. 1740. Yeigoro. Called also Mitsunari. A pupil of Inagawa Yoshikatsu, and a skilled expert. Yedo.

Yoshimune. 19th cent. Metal-worker of Yedo. Art name, Hiyaku-ji-ken.

Yoshinaga. Wao. 1740. A Yedo expert, who worked in the style of Yoshitsugu Kohei.

Yoshinaga. Yasui. 1660. Sahei. A pupil of Goto Mitsusadt Riujo. A great expert. Kyoto.

Yoshinaga. Tamagawa. 1780. Saburohei; also called Bumpei. One of the greatest of the Mito artists. Mito (Hitachi).

Yoshinaga. Furukawa. 1650. Sahei. A pupil of Goto Riujo. A fine artist. Kyoto.

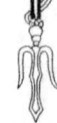

Yoshinaga. Umetada. 1650. Shichizayemon. One of the early Umetada workers. His tsuba are solid but of various shapes; some are chiselled à jour. A few have gold inlaying in the nunome style. Yoshinaga used the ideograph *ume* in marking his work. Vide Muneyuki.

Yoshinari. Ogawa. 1840. Minosuke. A pupil of Jikosai. Yedo.

Yoshinobu. 1750. Called himself Hi-yaku-ju-ken and marked his works Yoshinobu. A very skilled expert. Yedo.

Yoshinori. Yoshishige. 1630. Shokuro. Pupil of Yoshishige Gorosaku. Kaga.

Yoshinori. Mizuno. 1630. Genji. Kaga. Founder of the Mizuno family. A pupil of Goto Yenjo (Mitsuhide).

Yoshinori. Tsuji. 1780. Shinshiro. Art name, Yeisendo. An expert of the very highest skill. Worked in Omi. Also called Kariuken.

Yoshinori. Seki. 1820. Naokichi. Art name, Soriusai. A great artist. Yedo. Called also Umino Yoshinori.

Yoshioka. Family name. Vide Shigetsugu.

Yoshisada. Goto. 1630. Saijiro. Kaga.

Yoshisato. Ishiguro. 1850. Called himself Jitekisai. Nagasaki.

Yoshishige. Mizuno. 1630. Genji. A pupil of Goto Yenjo and very skilled. Kaga.

Yoshishige. 1620. Gorosaku. Brother of the celebrated Kuninaga of Kaga and pupil of Goto Tokujo. Gorosaku and his elder brother, Jirosaku are equally famous. Their works are commonly spoken of as Gorosaku-bori and Jirosaku-bori, and they are regarded as the originators of the Kaga school of experts. Gorosaku is said to have been taught painting by the artist, Sosa. He and his brother, Jirosaku, received an annual allowance of fifty bags of rice each from the feudal chief of Kaga.

His descendants, his pupils and their descendants took the name Yoshishige as a family name.

Yoshitada. 1840. Chiuzaburo. A pupil of Jikosai. Yedo.

Yoshitaka. Ishiguro. 1850. Kintaro. Yedo. Teacher of the celebrated Nara Yasuchika, and a great expert. Worked at Shonai in Dewa. He was followed by his son of the same name.

Yoshitake. Shoami. 1660. Tsutsui. A pupil of Sōden. (Ed. Sōten) Worked at Hikone.

Yoshitane. Honjo. 1850. Kamenosuke. A celebrated expert of Yedo, skilled not only as a sword-maker, but also as a chiseller of sword-mounts. One of the greatest workers of the nineteenth century.

Yoshitatsu. Fujiwara. Metal-worker of Yedo. Art names, Tessai and Tanzando.

Yoshiteru. Sonobe. 1840. Art name, Togindo. A skilled expert of Kyoto.

Yoshitsugu. Sakai. 1850. Sakujiro. Yedo.

Yoshitsugu. Shoami. 1800. Jiyemon. An expert of Aizu.

Yoshitsugu. Okamoto. 1760. To-no-shin. An elaborate carver with a wide range of designs, being himself a painter. Hagi.

Yoshitsugu. Yoshishige. 1740. Hachitayu. Kaga.

Yoshitsugu. Akao. 1640. Gonzayemon. First expert of the Akao family. Lived at Fukui in Yechizen. Worked in the Kinai style.

Yoshitsugu. Akao. 1670. Kohei or Kichiji. Celebrated as the first to apply pierced decoration to guards of shakudo. Born in Yechizen, but worked in Yedo. Commonly known as Kinai Kichiji.

Yoshitsugu. Akao. 1720. A tolerably skilled expert who worked in the style of Yoshitsugu Kohei. Yedo.

Yoshitsune. Ishiguro. 1850. Ginnosuke. Grandson of Jimiyo. Called himself Senyushi, Gammon and Tominsai. A celebrated expert. Yedo.

Yoshitsumu. 1830. A fine expert of Tokyo, teacher of Toriusai.

Yoshiyasu. Kato. 1670. Jihei. Kyoto

Yoshiyuki. Kumagaye. 1820. Employed by the Hosokuwa Daimiyo, for whom he carved a celebrated silver vase encircled by a bronze dragon. Worked in Yedo, and attained great repute.

Yoshiyuki. Akao. 1750. A Yedo expert, who worked in the style of Yoshitsugu Kohei.

Yoshōdō. Vide Masayasu.

Yozaburo. Yokoya. 19th cent. Metal-worker of Yanagawa. Called also Tomotsune.

Yūjō. Goto. 1460. The first of the great Goto Masters. Kyoto.

Yuki. Vide Masaya.

Yukinaga. Fujii. 1720. Gembei. His sword-mounts are profusely and delicately chiselled. Hagi.

Yukinao. Nakahara. 1710. Kichibei. Kyoto. Founder of the Nakahara family.

Yukinori. Nakahara. 1760. Kichibei. Called in his youth Yukhisia. A celebrated artist. It was his custom to carve all the mountings of a sword with designs en-suite. He moved from Kyoto to Nagato, by invitation of the Prince of Choshiu, and thenceforth worked in Hagi.

Yukitada. Nakahara. 19th cent. Metal-worker of Choshiu.

Yukitaka. Fujii. 1750. Genyemon. An artist of high repute. Son of Yukinaga (Fujii), he carved in the elaborate style of his father, but with more spirit. Hagi.

Yukitoshi. Nakahara. 1780. Genzayemon. Son of Yukinori, and scarcely inferior to his father. He also attained to considerable repute as a painter. Hagi.

Yukiyoshi. Nakahara. 1800. Hambei. Hagi.

Yūkotei. Vide Masanori.

Yūmeishi. Vide Muneaki.

Yūmin. Vide Teruaki (Yokoya).

Yurōsai. Vide Sekibun.

Yūsen. Vide Hiyobu Hogen.

Yushinto. Vide Tomobumi.

Zaisui. Funada. 1720. Shohachi. Teacher of the celebrated Nara Yasuchika, and a great expert. Worked at Shonai in Dewa. He was followed by his son of the same name.

Zeju. Iwamoto. 1830. Pupil of Iwamoto Konkwan. Yedo.

Zembei. Shibaya. 1750. A skilled inlayer of Sendai.

Zenjin. 1700. Date uncertain. Some fine specimens of his work exist, marked Akashi Yechizen.

Zenjo. Goto. 1600. Mitunari, or Kihei. Kyoto.

Zenjo. Goto. 1650. Mitsunori. Kyoto.

Zenshiro. 1610. A carver of Satsuma. Pupil of the Goto family.

Addendum:

Ed. Bushiu & Choshiu are now Bushu & Choshu, Soami to Shoami, other names are likewise now changed over time. 'Kwanto-gata', or Canton style is now known more commonly as Nanban [*Namban*]. Many words used in the text are hyphenated, this has been retained, but are no longer in modern usage. *Sōden* a sword-maker is throughout confused with *Sōten* the tsuba chiseller. Some references state that the artists are still living in "present day" however the original publication was in 1902 and even Natsuo, last of the great chisellers was already dead in 1898.

Abbreviated terms used:

à jour : -of or relating to objects that are pierced, perforated, or decorated with an openwork pattern. [Sukashi]

chefs-d'oeuvre : -Masterpiece, greatest work of a person's career.

Odile : -an amazing talented person, if sometimes a little odd.

Vide : -refer also to, -see also.

www.ingramcontent.com/pod-product-compliance
Lightning Source LLC
Chambersburg PA
CBHW060405290526
45791CB00002B/620